With Sincerest Appreciation to:

Jie Li, Kimberly Fu-hsing Tang, and Shirley Branch for artistic support and research

Dana Lynne Tang for spiritual support

Arlington Writers Group for critical critique and morale support

Forward

Within these pages, you will find an anthology of Chinese myths, legends, fables, and historical anecdotes. These are ancient stories that have been retold with relish by generations of grandfathers to their attentive audience. They are well-known to the Chinese, but seldom heard outside of Chung Kuo (The Middle Kingdom, the name Chinese gave their country.) They represent the essence of Chinese culture. The Chinese consider themselves as a nation of Rituals and Etiquette.

Parents and teachers use these stories as instruments for instilling moral fiber into their charges. Readers will find much pleasure and meaning in these tales while gaining an insight into the Dragon Kingdom (China) and its people.

Fables of the Dragon

Tales of China
Long Tang

GOLDEN FLEECE PRESS

Copyright © 2018 by Long Tang

All rights reserved. No part of this publication may be reproduced, distributed, or transmitted in any form or by any means, including photocopying, recording, or other electronic or mechanical methods, without the prior written permission of the publisher, except in the case of brief quotations embodied in critical reviews and certain other noncommercial uses permitted by copyright law. For permission requests, write to the publisher, addressed "Attention: Permissions Coordinator," at the address below.

Golden Fleece Press
PO Box 1464,
Centreville, VA 20122
www.goldenfleecepress.com

Special discounts are available on quantity purchases by corporations, associations, and others. For details, contact the publisher at the address above.

Epub ISBN 13: 978-1-942195-52-8
Mobi ISBN 13: 978-1-942195-53-5
Print ISBN 13: 978-1-942195-51-1
Pdf ISBN 13: 978-1-942195-54-2

Printed in the United States of America

First Edition

10 9 8 7 6 5 4 3 2 1

TABLE OF CONTENTS

Part I: The Book of Myths

1.	Nu Wa, The Goddess of Life	1
2.	Guan Yin, The Goddess of Mercy	4
3.	Chang Erh, The Goddess of the Moon	8
4.	The Chinese New Year	16
5.	The Chinese Horoscope	21
6.	The Emperor and the Dragon King	29
7.	The Old Man Under the Moon	49
8.	The Cowboy and the Seamstress	60
9.	The Dragon Mythology	70

Part II: The Book of Ladies

10.	Lu Hou, The First Empress	75
11.	Wu Ze Tian, The Female Emperor	80
12.	Ci Xi, The Last Ruler of Imperial China	86
13.	Mo Xi, The Temptress	91
14.	Da Ji, The Cruel Queen	93
15.	Bo She, The Smile That Toppled a Kingdom	96
16.	Li Ji, The Schemer	99
17.	Xi Shi, The Sunken Fish	102

18.	Wang Zhao Jun, The Fallen Geese	105
19.	Diao Chan, The Hidden Moon	108
20.	Yang Yu Huan, The Wilted Flower	111
21.	Princess Wen Cheng, The Queen of Tibet	114
22.	Zhong-Li Chun, The Ugly Queen	116
23.	The Three Moves of Lady Meng	119
24.	The Roar of the He-Dong Lioness	121
25.	Yehenala Buxiyamala, The Calamity Princess	123
26.	Chen Yuan-Yuan, The Dirge Siren	127

Part III: The Book of Fables

27.	The Wall of a Dream	133
28.	The Victory Chorus	135
29.	Fortunes in a Horse Lost	137
30.	The Fisherman's Catch	140
31.	Good Will	145
32.	Chou Chu and the Three Great Evils	152
33.	Life in Seven Paces	162
34.	The Price of Honor and Integrity	164
35.	Duan Wu, the Fifth of May Dragon Boat Festival	167

Part IV: The Book of Lore

36.	A Lesson in Etiquette	173
37.	The Tao of Tea	181
38.	The Imperial Champion	185
39.	The Chinese Ambassador	201
40.	The Beggar's Chicken	204
41.	A Lasting Prayer	209

Part I

The Book of Myths

1

NU WA, THE GODDESS OF LIFE

Pan Gu, the God of Creation, made the Heaven and the earth. After completing the task he laid down to rest and his body disintegrated to form the sun, the moon, stars, mountains, and rivers. A long time later, Fu Xi and Nu Wa appeared onto the world. They were brother and sister, with human heads and snakelike bodies.

Nu Wa felt the barrenness of the land and decided to create some companions. She was able to create as many as seventy different species of life in a day. On the first day, she kneaded mud into chickens and other fowl; on the second day, she made dogs, then goats on the third day, and pigs on the fourth day. She created oxen on the fifth day, then horses on the day after, before she made men and women into her own image on the seventh day.

Creating people individually by hand became tedious. After some thought, Nu Wa took a vine and whipped it at the mud she had been working with. Wherever the splattering mud landed a person popped into existence. Nu

Wa gathered the people and established the rules for marriages—with the women minding the home and the men providing for their livelihood. The Chinese especially revered Nu Wa for giving guidance to the people; they often depicted her holding a compass, signifying her role as the rule giver.

At the time, the world was shaped like a house, with the Heaven as its roof supported by tall mountains at each of the four corners. In the Heaven above the world, lived the Jade Emperor who ruled the celestial realm with his staff of minor deities in attendance. One day, Gong Gong the God of Water, got drunk at a banquet given by the Jade Emperor and had an argument with Zhu Rong, the God of Fire. The altercation led to violence and the inebriated God of Water lost the ensuing fight. In a fit of shameful rage, the sore loser smashed his head against the mountain that held up the western corner of the Heaven. The tall mountain cracked and split then crumbled. It created a gaping hole in that part of the Heaven and a chasm in the earth. Fire from underground ignited the forests, animals fled from the woods into the farm fields and devoured crops and people. At the same time, water from the giant hole in the western mountain inundated the earth like a great flood. Earth became a purgatory filled with the dead and the dying.

Faced with the horrible disaster, Nu Wa canvassed the world and gathered 36,501 five-colored stones and smelted them into a paste she used to patch the hole in the western sky. It took four years to patch the broken ceiling in the Heaven. She used up all except one piece of the stone, which still sat atop the Tian-Tai Mountain by the shore of the Eastern Ocean.

After repairing the sky, she cut a foot off of the Great Tortoise of the ocean and used it to replace the broken pillar at the western corner of the world. However, the tortoise leg was shorter than the giant post it had replaced; therefore the western Heaven ended up lower than the other parts of the world and that is why the sun, the moon, and the stars slide westward each day and night. The rainbows that appeared after a rainfall were reflections from Nu Wa's patchwork of the sky.

She also gathered large quantities of reeds and burnt them into ashes she used to sop up and dam the flood water into lakes. But she left two great canals to drain the flood water eastward into the ocean. The remnants of these waterways became the Yellow River and the Yangtze River.

At last, the people were able to survive the disaster. She made reed pipes from leftover reeds and taught people how to create music from them. This became known as the first Chinese musical instrument - *Sheng*.

To this date, Chinese revere Nu Wa as the most important goddess.

2

GUAN YIN, THE GODDESS OF MERCY

There are numerous versions of the story about Guan Yin, The Goddess of Mercy. The *Precious Scroll of Fragrant Mountain* (**香山寶卷**) describes an incarnation of Guan Yin as the daughter of a king who wanted her to marry a wealthy but unfeeling prince, who cared naught for the people.

King Miao Zhuang ordered his daughter, Princess Miao Shan, to get married. Initially, she refused to marry a man with no humility, eventually she agreed only if three conditions were satisfied. She would obey the king and marry the man who could alleviate the 'Three Great Miseries' of the people.

The exasperated king demanded to know the specifics of the Three Great Miseries that afflicted his people. Miao Shan listed the first misery as the suffering people endured as they age. The second misery was the aches people endured when they fell sick. And the third misery was the pain people endured at death. If the marriage could not ease all of the above then she would not marry and would instead devote her life to alleviating the suffering of the people.

When her father asked who could ease all of the above, Miao Shan responded that a physician would be able to do all of those things. Her father grew angry as he wanted her to marry a person of power and wealth, not a healer. He forced her to labor in the palace and reduced her food and drink but she did not change her mind.

The princess then asked to become a nun. The king eventually allowed her to work in the temple, but ordered the senior priest to give her the toughest chores. The monks forced Miao Shan to work all day and all night while others slept in order to finish her work. However, she was such a good person that the animals living around the temple began to help her with her chores. Her father learned about her helpers and became so frustrated that he set fire to the temple. Miao Shan put out the fire with her bare hands and suffered no burns. Struck with fear, her father ordered her to be put to death.

As the executioner swung his ax to carry out her father's orders, it shattered into a thousand pieces. He then tried a sword which likewise broke apart. He tried to shoot Miao Shan with arrows but they all veered around her. In desperation, he tried to use his hands to strangle the princess. Miao Shan realized the fate that the executioner would meet at her father's hand should she fail to die and she allowed herself to be killed. She then forgave the executioner, and voluntarily assumed the great karmic guilt the executioner generated for killing her, thus leaving him guiltless.

When Miao Shan's spirit descended into the realm of Hell, she witnessed the suffering and horrors that the beings there endured and was overwhelmed with grief. Filled with compassion, she released all the good karma she had accumulated through her many lifetimes and freed numerous suffering souls back into the Heaven and Earth. In the process, she converted hell into paradise. King Yen Lo, the ruler of hell, sent her back to the human world to prevent the utter destruction of his realm, and she arrived on Fragrant Mountain (Xiang Shan 香山).

King Miao Zhuang fell ill and no physician was able to cure him. A monk visited the palace and claimed that the king's illness could be cured by making a potion from the arm and eyes of one of his daughters. The two older daughters of the king refused to make the sacrifice. The monk then told the king about a goddess at Fragrant Mountain that might be able to cure him of the illness. The king arrived at Fragrant Mountain only to find the goddess was his deceased daughter. When Miao Shan learned of the king's ailment and the remedy, she cut off her arm and gouged out her own eyes without hesitation.

When the king recovered, he prayed to the gods to give back the arm and eyes to his daughter. Miao Shan's merciful kindness stirred the gods, and they rewarded her with a thousand eyes and a thousand pairs of arms. The appreciative king built a temple atop the Fragrant Mountain to honor Miao Shan and bestowed on her the name of Goddess Guan Yin of a Thousand Arms.

Miao Shan was about to ascend into Heaven when she heard cries of woe from the world below. She turned and saw the great suffering endured by the people on earth. Filled with compassion, she returned to the human realm, vowing never to leave until such time as all suffering had ended.

The belief in Goddess Guan Yin originated from Buddhism, and the image of Guan Yin has transformed over the ages. Early images of Guan Yin were male figures and to this date, there are some male images of Guan Yin in temples of Asia. During the Chinese Song Dynasty, Daoism dominated the realm. By imperial decree, Buddhist gods were transferred and became Daoist deities. Despite the transformation, Guan Yin remained a most revered deity of the

Chinese people because she swore to remain on earth until all sufferings of the people had been alleviated.

3
CHANG ERH, THE GODDESS OF THE MOON

The Goddess of the Moon was a beautiful lady who risked her life to save her people. She gave us the Full Moon Festival, one of the oldest holidays celebrated by the people of the Dragon Kingdom. She lived in an era when gods frequently mingled with mortals, and man could achieve deity status through meditation, herbal medicine or the performance of great selfless deeds.

In the realm above the earth, ten Suns lived in the Fountain of the Heaven, bathing in its cool water when not patrolling the skies. They took turns, once every ten days, roaming the earth, generating warmth, light, and energy for all beings. They were the sons of the Jade Emperor, responsible for providing life force to the world.

The Jade Emperor decreed that no more than one Sun would soar in the sky at any time. But, spending nine out of every ten days in the Fountain of the Heaven became a boring routine. Each of the brothers wished for more time to parade proudly through the Heaven and bath in the ardor and admiration of the people. Each Sun jealously guarded his allotted time in the sky. Whenever one fell ill, he would not allow another to take his place, which explained the infrequent solar eclipses.

One night, Golden Wheel, the oldest and the most powerful of the Suns, called his nine brothers to a meeting. At his urging, the ten brothers agreed to band together and defy the edict of their father. It would be fun to play together, and show the people the greatness of their clan!

The next morning, they soared together into the Heaven, and the people awakened to the combined might of ten solar beings. The Suns played tag and other games, frolicking across the sky. Their antics left broad, charred swaths of earth. Rivers and lakes boiled dry, crops and animals died from thirst and heat. People suffered and perished by the thousands from famine and the scorching heat.

Cries for help pierced the clouds and reached the Heavenly Palace. Squadrons of Imperial Guards of the Heaven responded in swarms of cloud chariots to curb the ten errant brothers. The Guards quickly herded the brother together at the bank of the great Milky Way, where the ten Suns banded as one to face their pursuers. The combined solar energy of the ten suns easily evaporated the chariots and fried the Imperial Guards, turning them into flashing streams of meteors. The jubilant brothers returned triumphantly to their playground in the sky and celebrated with a parade over the earth.

The death and suffering of the people and the utter impotence of the Imperial Guards outraged Hou Yi, the mightiest hunter of the land. He vowed to do that which the gods could not. His strength and skill in archery, unmatched even by the gods, became the last hope of the people. While Hou Yi prepared his weapons, his wife Chang Erh held back her tears and hid her anxiety over the dangerous venture. It would be difficult enough for a mortal to face one deity, but to fight ten at once was beyond foolhardiness. But, it would be disloyal and dishonorable for her to stand in his way, especially when the fate of all people hung in the balance.

At the door, Chang Erh forced a smile to her haggard face and draped a cloth bundle over Hou Yi's right shoulder. "Some cured meat and buns to sustain you through your ordeal," she said bravely. No pleading words to stay his feet; she must not dull his fighting spirit with tender words, they could mean the difference between success and failure.

Hou Yi looked at his wife's beautiful oval face and reached over to wipe a lock of sweat-stained hair pasted to her brow. A thousand words of tender affection passed unspoken between them as his fingers touched her tresses. At length, he withdrew his callused hand. With a curt parting nod accompanied by a masculine grunt, Hou Yi marched down the path with not a backward glance.

Chang Erh's eyes followed the receding figure of her husband, she then fell to her knees and prayed to the gods that protection and assistance be given to her husband. Moved by her loyal devotion to her husband and her people, the local hearth god quickly delivered her prayer to the Heavenly Palace. The Jade Emperor, fuming with outrage at the humiliating defeat of his guards at the hands of his own sons, decided to atone for the shame with the ultimate sacrifice of a father. He dispatched a messenger to deliver a glittering bronze quiver containing ten shining ebony arrows to Hou Yi. The missiles had been fashioned by Lǚ Pan, the god of all tools, including weaponry. Their tips were fashioned from fingers nails of the Jade Emperor, capable of killing all things, be it mortal or deity.

Hou Yi climbed to the top of the tall and craggy Yellow Mountain and gauged the flight paths of the ten blazing fireballs above. The unsuspecting culprits continued roaming the sky, leaving carpets of flame and smoldering ashes over the land. Eventually, their horseplay brought them near the majestic peak. Hou Yi waited until the heat started to melt the rocks, then let fly his first arrow. Without waiting to see the result of his shot, he quickly loosed two more missiles into the sky.

His first salvo hit their marks and three Suns glowed into darkness and turned into black crows as they tumbled from the sky. The other seven Suns were startled; but, before they could recover, three more of their number flared and turned into dead crows. In a panic, the remaining four Suns fled in different directions, kindling walls of flame in their wakes to impede their predator. Hou Yi leaped off his perch on the mountain and gave chase. The Jade Emperor sent the Thunder God and the Rain Goddess to aid him in the task. A torrential rain poured from of the sky to douse the fires and cool a path for Hou Yi to continue his pursuit.

Despite the immensity of the great open sky, the fugitive Suns could not outrace Hou Yi's arrows. One after another, three more of the remaining Suns blazed in agony then darkened and fell from the sky, leaving only Golden Wheel cringing behind the Moon. The resulting eclipse plunged the earth into darkness, providing a much-needed relief to the land. The proximity of the Sun to the Moon boiled its surface, leaving a forever-cratered moonscape.

Hou Yi blinked to adjust his eyes to the darkness then notched his last arrow against the bowstring to take aim at the lone trembling Sun. Suddenly, the archer felt a strong wave of gentleness wash over him. He turned sideways and found the Holy Buddha standing serenely next to him. A luminous aura surrounded and poured forth from the body of that celestial deity. The almighty God of Mercy and Humanity raised his right hand to his chest and gently spoke, "Blessed is all that is merciful, brave warrior. Please spare the last remaining Sun. There has been enough killing for one day. The people need the Sun's light to work, its heat for warmth, and energy to give life to the crops in the fields."

It was only then that Hou Yi realized the cause of the darkness enveloping the world, and saw the merit of the Holy Buddha's advice. He relaxed his bow and returned the last magical arrow to his quiver. "As you say, Your Holiness." Then Hou Yi turned toward Golden Wheel with the bow raised and shouted, "It is by the grace of the Holy Buddha that you have been spared. I shall keep this last arrow. If you should again violate the Law of the Heaven, I will return and send you to join your brothers." Golden Wheel moved slowly and hesitantly out from behind his makeshift shield. He sent forth rays of heat to dry up the drenched land, and everything returned to normal.

Survivors, human and animal emerged from their caverns, extremely grateful to Hou Yi for his accomplishment. They danced and sang praise to Hou Yi's success. The King immediately appointed their savior as General of the Army. When the old King approached death, he acceded to the will of the people, renouncing his throne in favor of Hou Yi.

Unfortunately, Hou Yi lacked the necessary training and experience to be a good ruler. Although a good hunter, he had no knowledge of kingship. He ignored his responsibilities to the people and devoted his time to the pursuit of joy and luxury. Hou Yi's extravagance quickly emptied the national treasury, causing increased taxes and widespread poverty to his people. His great and frequent hunting parties quickly emptied the land of game and mere survival became a difficult task for the people.

Eventually, his subjects rebelled, but war and fighting were things Hou Yi excelled at and enjoyed. He personally led the army against the rebel forces. In the end, no rebel leader survived against Hou Yi's arrows, and the rebellions were ruthlessly crushed.

Although the rebels failed to topple Hou Yi from the throne, they caused him to think about the frailty of his existence. When he became old and feeble, he would not be able to stamp out challenges to his throne. He needed a way to stave off the advancement of age. In the ensuing years, Hou Yi summoned the best alchemists and physicians to his court. He demanded an elixir of eternal life. Legions of herbalists canvassed all corners of the world, seeking ingredients for the task. To ensure their return, Hou Yi held family members of the herbalists as hostages.

Legend had it that one herbalist convinced Hou Yi to give him five hundred boys and five hundred girls as gifts to the gods to exchange for the Fruit of Eternal Life. The herbalist took the children across the Eastern Seas and founded the nation of Japan, with himself as Emperor of the Land of the Rising Sun.

After decades of hard work, the alchemists, at last, had sufficient ingredients for the elixir. As the date of completion neared, Hou Yi ordered preparations for a grand celebration. At the height of the festivities, Hou Yi and his favorite wives and concubines would assemble atop a specially constructed pavilion. Then, in full view of all the people, they would each take a dose of the magical potion, and thus attain immortality and rule the Kingdom for eternity.

Chang Erh despaired at Hou Yi's tyranny. Repeated pleading and counseling only nettled her husband, causing estrangement between the two. She thought, *if Hou Yi should gain eternal life, the people would be condemned to suffer forever under a cruel tyrant*. Thirty-odd years ago, Chang Erh had been willing to sacrifice her husband for the good of the people. Fate once again called upon her to sacrifice for the good of the people; but this time, she must betray her king and husband.

On the eve before the planned festivities, Chang Erh sneaked into the royal bedchamber and removed the sacred black arrow from Hou Yi's quiver. The palace guards recognized the arrow as Hou Yi's symbol of authority and allowed Chang Erh to pass into the alchemist's laboratory. She quickly found the gourd containing the potion of eternity and made her escape. Unfortunately, the thievery was discovered before Chang Erh could escape from the palace. Gongs crashed and alarm bells rang, as guards and night watchmen hurried to report the news to the King.

Through the commotion, she clearly heard the familiar but frantic voice of Hou Yi, as he ordered the palace gates be sealed, and the men assembled to search for Chang Erh and the missing potion.

Chang Erh found herself trapped in the central palace, and was forced to flee into the newly built pavilion, the stage of the next day's celebrations. From the balcony at the top of the building, she saw snaking lines of torches roaming the palace grounds, while others ringed the gates and the battlements. Chang Erh spotted Hou Yi and a detachment of bodyguards as they drew near the pavilion. Faced with imminent capture, Chang Erh decided to drink the entire potion in the gourd, to prevent Hou Yi from getting it. While one small dose of the potion would give any recipient eternal life, such a large amount would surely kill her. Still, it would prevent Hou Yi from becoming an eternal tyrant. He would surely die of old age before all the necessary ingredients could be gathered again for a new batch of the elixir to be brewed.

Approaching footsteps on the stairs alerted Chang Erh to the proximity of her pursuers; she tilted the gourd and drained its entire contents down her own throat. She gagged on the bitter liquid, as not a few drops ran down her cheeks to drip onto her gown. Just when she had choked down the last drop of potion, Hou Yi stepped from the stairway onto the balcony. He gave a shout and dashed forward to grab Chang Erh. She launched herself into the air, intending to atone for her disloyalty by committing suicide. But, instead of hurtling toward the ground, she found herself floating up and away from the palace.

Everyone gasped in surprise at the fairy-like figure floating under the moonlight. Some people thought they were in the presence of a goddess and knelt to pay their respects. Hou Yi quickly recovered his wits, and immediately sent for an archer.

By the time the man arrived with the bow and arrows, Chang Erh had dwindled to the size of a tiny doll, rising ever higher in the bright moonlit sky. Nevertheless, with one smooth practiced draw, Hou Yi let fly with his arrow at the shrinking figure. Perhaps age and prolonged luxury had taken their toll on Hou Yi's body, or it could have been the lingering sentiment for Chang Erh that caused his hands to tremble; whatever the reason, for the first time in his adult life, Hou Yi missed his target. By this time, the entire population had turned out to watch as Chang Erh shrunk to the size of a pea then disappeared into the face of the Moon.

Chang Erh's sudden arrival on the Moon surprised the local deities. Unable to decide what to do with their uninvited guest, they welcomed her to their home and sent a messenger to advise the Heavenly Palace of the event. At length, the Jade Emperor decided Chang Erh should remain in the Heavenly realm. In recognition of her self-sacrifice for the people, the Jade Emperor appointed her as Goddess of the Moon.

Since then, every August 15th, the Chinese celebrate the Full Moon Festival by eating round moon cakes and recounting the story of Chang Erh. The golden egg yolk inside a bed of black bean paste symbolizes the moon against the dark night sky.

The Chinese lunar space program is named The Chang Erh Program.

4
THE CHINESE NEW YEAR

Everything must start with a beginning. What better way to launch a story than to recount the origin of the Chinese New Year. Also known as the Spring Festival, it is the longest and the most important of all Chinese holidays. All Chinese people and countless others throughout the world observe this holiday. While it has no religious significance, it is a celebration of continuity and family life, dedicated to harmony and prosperity. To the Chinese, the occasion represents the time when everyone becomes one year older–age is calculated by the year, not the date of birth.

Everyone knows that a Chinese New Year celebration starts with a bang (of firecrackers). Legend has it that early in the era of human existence a monster would appear at the end of the winter to devour villagers. With a valiant effort, the people would drive off the monster with bright torches and loud noises, which evolved into the firecracker celebrations of today.

However, preparations for the Spring Festival start long before lighting the fuses of explosive devices. Like many ancient civilizations, the Chinese society is replete with superstitions. In the case of the Chinese, symbolism merges with superstition to play a significant role in its society.

Near the end of the final month of the year, all families begin cleaning, then cooking food for offerings to ancestors and Gods. On the 24th day of the 12th month, the Kitchen God of each household departs the earth to relate, to the Jade Emperor in Heaven, the deeds of each family during the past year.

A family's fortune for the coming year rests with the report by the Kitchen God. A virtuous family will be rewarded, while those who have misbehaved will receive misfortunes.

People resort to various measures to ensure a prosperous New Year. Some families bribe the Kitchen God with sweets, so he will say sweet (good) words about them. Others try to silence the Kitchen God by offering him sticky rice cakes, so as to glue his mouth shut. Many people make offerings of potent wine in the hope of getting the Kitchen God inebriated so that he cannot deliver accurate accounts of their misdeeds. The goal is to take preventive maintenance measures, avoid unpleasantness, and start the New Year on a good note.

The purpose of the major housecleaning is to sweep away bad luck, so as not to carry it into the New Year. Fresh flowers and red papers decorate the household, giving it a healthy and vibrant look. Red is an eye-catching color and denotes greatness. People, especially children, don new clothing with red as the dominant color. Miniature orange trees and jade plants are also favorite decorations around the house. The bright yellow oranges symbolize gold, the precious metal and, combined with the much-coveted jade, represent prosperity. The jade is also valued for its mythical power to ward off evil spirits. The word "fortune" is written on red paper, and hung upside down on the exterior door;

this is because the word for "upside down" in Chinese is phonetically synonymous with the word "arrive" - thus, "fortune" arrives into the household.

Cooking large amounts of food is necessary to ensure plenty of leftovers, signifying that the coming year will be a year of plenty. One frequently-prepared dish is a whole fish because the Chinese word for "fish" sounds the same as the word for "abundance." A fish, with head and tail intact, symbolizes "plenty" from the beginning of the year to its end.

On New Year's Eve, regardless of distance, a person must make it home for the family reunion; all shops and offices are closed so employees can be home for the traditional dinner feast. After a sumptuous multi-course meal, family members gather to tell stories, exchange the latest news about friends and relatives, and catch up on events of the past year. For some families, it is the only time of the year when everyone sees each other. It is also not unusual for the entire family to gamble and play games throughout the night, and the children are allowed to stay up late with the adults. Firecrackers, bright lights and loud noises are encouraged to scare off evil spirits and to portend a lively New Year.

Early in the morning on New Year's Day, children pay respect to their parents, who in return hand out red envelopes containing money as gifts. Doors are opened wide to welcome "Good Fortune". Special care is taken not to utter negative words, such as bad luck, death, sickness, or poverty. No housecleaning is allowed, to avoid sweeping "Good Fortune" away. Scissors and knives are hidden, so as not to cut up "Good Fortune" by mistake. Whatever happens during these first few days will set the tone for the remainder of the year.

During this first day, many families do not cook; they enjoy warmed-over food from the previous evening's feast. Some families abstain from eating meat during this time of the year, so as to allow the animals - furred, finned and feathered—to also have an opportunity to celebrate the New Year.

This is obviously a good time for children to make demands on their parents as their requests are seldom denied! Anything negative is to be avoided. The same can be said of beggars seeking alms. They too get to benefit from the festivities.

Lastly, on this day, families visit friends and relatives on the paternal side to exchange New Year's greetings, gifts and red envelopes of money for the children.

Lion and dragon dances are prevalent in the streets on New Year's Day. Dragons are the spirits of rain and abundance and are welcomed by the people who need water for a good harvest. The lion is the symbol of prosperity; thus lion dancers are especially welcomed by merchants, who hold red envelopes of money for the dancers to grasp with their lions' mouths. Sometimes, the lion dancers must prance through a gauntlet of exploding firecrackers and perform acrobatic feats to seize red envelopes placed in elevated locations.

On the second day of the New Year, families visit friends and relatives on the maternal side, and on the third day, everyone remains home as the Gods of Anger and Bad Luck take their turn to roam the streets. On the fourth day, the Kitchen God returns, and a new picture of him is hung on the wall. For merchants and offices, it is normal business as usual after the return of the Kitchen God. The seventh day of the New Year honors the creation of mankind, and friends gather for banquets to celebrate the occasion. The ninth day is the birthday of the Jade Emperor and festive events are said to be conducted in honor of the occasion.

The Spring Festival officially ends on the 15th day of the first month of the year with the celebration of the Lantern Festival, commemorating the first full moon of the New Year. Communities hold competitions for the prettiest and most ingeniously designed lanterns. In modern days, lantern float parades take place in some cities. Some people conclude their celebrations by floating small candlelit boats on rivers, ponds, and creeks to help light up the New Year. Thus, with such an auspicious beginning, the Chinese are well prepared to face the coming "New Year".

5
THE CHINESE HOROSCOPE

The Chinese horoscope, steeped in the legends and fables of The Middle Kingdom, form a unique part of the Chinese culture. Like the Western Zodiac, the Chinese horoscope has twelve signs, with a specific symbol to represent personalities of the individual, and govern his or her relationship with others. The Chinese horoscope differs from its western counterpart in that it runs in twelve-year cycles, as opposed to a monthly rotation (of the western horoscope). In addition, a rank order delineates the hierarchy within the Chinese horoscope. The story of the Chinese horoscope is one of the oldest and most popular tales in the Land of the Dragon.

High above the majestic eastern mountains, the glittering multi-tiered Heavenly Palace floated on a bed of gold and silver clouds. Within that palace, the Jade Emperor sat in judgment over all things living and dead—gods, ghosts, mortals, animals, fowls and marine life. Subordinate to the Jade Emperor, countless demigods governed their assigned realms.

The Imperial Council of the Heavens had just completed work on the grand design for the human horoscope, to delineate the characters and traits of mortals. The time had come to appoint 12 creatures as representative symbols of the horoscope. The wily Minister of the Exalted White-Golden Star, supported by a host of junior spirits, proposed a slate of animals, headed by the cunning fox, to represent each sign of the horoscope.

The ingenious Minister of the Seven Northern Stars and his cast of demigods countered with a list of his favorite avian candidates, led by the sage and elegant crane.

Thunder rolled, lightning flashed, and the earth trembled for 12 days and nights. The Heavenly Palace of the Clouds reverberated from the shock waves of the heated debate. Tired of the ceaseless bickering, the Jade Emperor waved his scepter to end the controversy, and at the same time demonstrated his divine wisdom and diplomatic tact. He rejected both lists and decreed a novel selection process.

At dawn of the next day, scores of imperial messengers of the Heavens commandeered puffs of silvery cloud chariots, to deliver the Jade Emperor's proclamation to the world:

"It is the wish of the Imperial Jade Emperor to select 12 creatures as symbols for the human horoscope. All who desire to become a sign of the horoscope must travel to the Heavenly Temple atop the majestic Yellow Mountain. The first twelve animals to arrive shall earn a place in the eternal horoscope. The order of arrival at the Heavenly Temple shall determine the hierarchy of the winners."

At this point in history, the Cat and the Rat were neighbors and the best of friends. They had been walking toward home when they saw, standing on a burst of silvery cloud in the bright blue sky, an imperial herald who announced the Heavenly edict. The pair was at first surprised, then excited as they realized the significance of the proclamation. It would mean eternal honor for the clans of the chosen dozen.

Both animals decided to compete for a place in the horoscope. They immediately rushed homeward to prepare for the trip. As they approached their village, the calculating feline very casually swished his long furry tail and slowly rolled his slanted golden eyes downward to glance at his rat companion, Lao Shu. "Little brother, how should we decide on the horoscope ranking between us, once we get to the Heavenly Temple?"

Noting the deep undertone in the Cat's voice, the Rat paused and carefully chose his words before offering a response. "Well, Amao. Since you are the older brother, it is only right that you should rank above me." He then gaped wide his pointed snout and faked a yawn before adding, "it is getting dark and we are tired. I suggest we rest for the night and make an early start in the morning."

Amao, the feline, became hypnotized by the yawn and suddenly felt a wave of fatigue wash over him. He arched his back then rubbed his eyes with his front paws. "Yes, you are right. A short rest will refresh us for the trip." Amao smugly lifted his tail to smooth a patch of ruffled fur along his spine. He continued as an afterthought, "since you usually sleep during the day and hunt for food at night, you probably won't be able to sleep anyway. Perhaps you could pack some food for us to eat on the road, while I take a nap? When you are ready, you can wake me, so that we can get started on the trip."

"As you wish, older brother, I shall take care of everything. Just go and have a good rest. I'll come and get you when I have packed the necessities for the trip." Lao Shu nervously twitched his whiskers and bowed to Amao, then crawled into the rat burrow. The Cat gave a casual wave of the tail and a nod in return and then continued on to his own den. He leaped into his bed, yawned, stretched and kneaded the bedding with his paws, then curled down to dream of his soon-to-be-gained place of honor in the horoscope.

Meanwhile, Lao Shu rushed about in his burrow to pack a bag of food for the trip. As the Rat rifled through the larder, he raged over the way Amao had browbeaten his way into the higher rank in the horoscope. *That Amao always uses his size and seniority to gain an advantage in our relationship. The fact that he is older, stronger and bigger only makes me want to rebel against his dominance.*

Lao Shu considered himself to be smarter than Amao, and in the past had been able to gain small advantages over the feline via wile and trickery. The Rat had always sought an opportunity to get back at Amao. *And now, the race for a spot in the horoscope presents the perfect opportunity for me to even the score once and for all,* thought Lao Shu. With his mind made up, he sneaked out to check on Amao in his den. The Rat crouched in the silent darkness and, over the pounding of his own heartbeat, heard a deep, rumbling purring from the Cat's lair. Quietly, Lao Shu tiptoed away from the cat's house then raced down the road toward the Heavenly Temple.

Dawn found Amao crawling out of his den. He had awakened in a cold sweat, having just had a nightmare about drowning in an ocean of water. Suddenly, noting the time of the day, the enraged Cat leaped up spitting and hissing, and rushed to Lao Shu's nest, only to discover that the Rat was gone. Amao screamed a frustrated howl then sped down the road to catch up with Lao Shu. Finally, in the distance, the Cat spied the diminutive figure of the Rat hunched over the bank of the rampaging Yellow River.

A sixth sense caused Lao Shu to glance back, what he saw sent a sudden involuntary shudder to course through his body. Lao Shu steeled himself to remain calm. With a twitch of his whiskers, he forced a toothy smile onto his face and then steeled himself to approach the obviously angry Amao with a boisterous greeting. "Older brother, I'm so glad you had come, you have saved me the trouble of coming to fetch you. I was pondering the problem of crossing the great Yellow River and decided to make an inspection to see if there was a way to ford it. As you can see, the river is too wide and fast for us to swim across. Perhaps you can think of a way to get us to the other side."

Lao Shu's composed disposition confused Amao and succeeded in deflecting his rage. The ego of the self-centered feline simply did not allow him to believe that the puny Rat would dare to double-cross him! With a disdainful swish of his tail, he signaled acceptance of the explanation given by the obsequious Rat.

The raging current of the Yellow River quickly captured the Cat's attention, as the memory of his recent nightmare flashed into mind. At length, he regained his composure and turned from the river to sneer condescendingly at his small friend. "It is a good thing that I woke up on my own. If I had to wait for you to wake me, the two of us would have arrived too late at the Heavenly Temple to earn our places in the horoscope." Happy to have the incident forgotten, Lao Shu mumbled flattering words of gratitude to appease the Cat, while the long tail worked itself forward to whisk away drops of cold sweat from above his beady eyes.

The pair searched for ways to cross the Yellow River, but it was just too wide and fast. With no bridge or ferry in sight, they needed a boat or a raft. To no avail, they frantically paced up and down the riverbank searching for someone or something to help them ford the river. Suddenly, the Rat spotted a giant shape amble toward them. Lao Shu quickly darted to the Cat's side and whispered in his ear, "Keep quiet and let me do the talking. I think I have just found a way to cross the river." Amao's anxiety and ambition caused him to overlook the Rat's insolence; the feline slapped his tail against the ground and nodded a doubtful consent.

"Good morning to you, Honorable Master Ox. Where are you going so early on this fine day?" squealed the Rat as the lumbering form of the giant water buffalo approached the riverbank.

The towering Ox stopped and turned his superbly horned head to search for the source of the voice. Finally, he looked down and found, standing between his two fore hoofs, a pair of small figures half hidden in the tall grass by the river bank. "Oh, good morning to you, little brothers. I'm on my way to the gathering for the horoscope selection. Since I travel at such a slow pace, I decided to start early so as to ensure myself a spot on the roster."

As the Cat bowed and fumbled for words to greet the Ox, Lao Shu hurriedly hopped atop a boulder to get at eye level with the Ox. "Oh, is that so Most Honorable Brother Ox? We had not heard of the gathering. We would surely have liked to join you, but my brother, Amao and I, are on our way to visit our families on the other side of the river. The recent storm has washed out the only bridge within a hundred li's and we are stuck on this side. Oh, brother Ox, in the name of the all-merciful Buddha, would you be so kind as to carry us across on your back?"

"I suppose so since I am headed in the same direction. Just hold on tight, so that you don't fall into the river." The kindly Ox then knelt to take aboard two passengers onto his broad shoulders.

"Thank you for being so kind," said the Rat. Then he turned to Amao. "Big Brother, I would be honored if you would ride in the front. Your greater height will help Brother Ox spot obstacles in the river." The Cat, pleased with the sense of humility demonstrated by Lao Shu, nodded smugly and sprang aboard the back of the giant Ox. The Rat quickly followed and grasped Amao's waist for stability.

The kindly Ox made sure the passengers were ready then walked into the fast flowing river. Torrents of rushing waves crashed at the flank of the big Ox, splashing the two passengers with the muddy brown water. The waves had little effect on the great Ox, but the awesome power and the noise of the magnificent river mesmerized the Cat. Images of the previous night's nightmare flashed across his mind. Unconsciously, Amao tightened his grips on the ox horns. Behind him, the Rat felt the tensing muscles of the furry feline and surmised the source of the Cat's anxiety. Lao Shu smiled as he mentally rehearsed every step of his scheme.

At midstream, Lao Shu nudged Amao on the shoulder with his pointed snout and shouted into the Cat's pinned back ears. Of course, the Rat's words lost all coherence in the deafening noise of the raging water. Finally, Lao Shu managed to shake Amao out of his trance. The feline unlocked his tight grip on the Ox's horns and leaned back to hear what the little brother had to say.

While the Cat teetered slightly off balance, Lao Shu dug the claws of his hind legs into the Ox's thick hide for leverage and bit Amao on the back of the neck. The sudden pain in the neck surprised Amao, made him jump and lose his grip on the horns. Lao Shu followed with a strong shove to the side, downstream. The feline screamed and clawed air as he tumbled into the raging torrent. The powerful current quickly pulled him under and carried him away from his travel companions.

Fortunately, Amao managed to reach out a claw and snare a large tree trunk that had been floating by and climbed aboard. At a bend in the river, he leaped to grasp an overhanging willow branch and struggled his way to shore. At length, the exhausted and wet feline shook off the water and started after the traitorous Rat.

Meanwhile, the great Ox did not even notice the lightened load on his back, as he easily reached the opposite shore of the Yellow River. Once ashore, Lao Shu quickly jumped off and left without even a word of gratitude to the Ox. The Rat raced all the way to the top of the Yellow Mountain, and, as the first animal to reach the Heavenly Temple, claimed the first place in the horoscope.

In spite of the slow plodding gait, the Ox had sufficient early start to take the second place.

Soon afterward, a thunderous roar announced the arrival of the Cat's cousin, the Tiger. Behind him, a bouncing rabbit leaped onto the scene. Then a giant shadow descended atop the Yellow Mountain. The elongated body and bright blue scales could belong to none other than the majestic Dragon. In spite of the fact that he lived in the distant ocean, his speed in flight had earned him the fifth place. As the Dragon landed in the temple courtyard, from one of his front talons, the Snake unwrapped itself to get on the ground and claim the sixth place. Apparently, he had wheedled a ride from his giant cousin.

Next, the Horse raced to reach the Heavenly Temple, just beating out the Goat by a nose. With a triumphant screech, the Monkey King swung down from a tree, a tad ahead of the giant Rooster, who crowed as he flew the last ten feet into the temple courtyard. Right behind them, the Dog snapped at the curly tail of the Boar, who dodged out of the way of the sharp teeth. The slight side step allowed the Dog to forge ahead and the Boar slipped into the last place.

Finally, Amao led an assortment of other animals onto the top of the mountain. Unfortunately for Amao and the others, the Boar had already taken the last place in the horoscope. The treachery of Lao Shu had cost Amao a place of honor for himself, and thus his clan.

It was at this point in the history of the universe that the Cat and the Rat ended their prolonged friendship. Ever since then, descendants of the Rat continue to pay the price of his betrayal. The Cats took to napping during the day, so they can hunt rats at night.

6

THE EMPEROR AND THE DRAGON KING

In Chinese mythology, the Jade Emperor of the Heaven ruled supreme over each and every part of the world. His subordinate gods and goddesses were masters of all things large and small, from a deep ocean or tall mountain to that of the doorway in a lowly hovel. Chinese gods are in many ways similar to the deities of Greek mythology, possessing the emotions and weaknesses of mere mortals. The whimsical acts of the deities can and do produce surprising and at times dire consequences, such is the case with the Dragon King of the Eastern Ocean.

In the deepest trenches of the Eastern Ocean, the Dragon King sat on a giant pearl-trimmed throne in the Water Crystal Palace. Every life form in the Eastern Ocean lived at the mercy of his whim. With his right front claws, the Dragon King stroked the two long, sinewy tentacles at the tip of his elongated snout and yawned in boredom, *there must be something I can do to break these doldrums*. Suddenly the two golden orbs that served as his eyes gleamed a shiny glow. *I know who can help me,* he thought. *The Old Tortoise has been living for over a millennium. He is ancient and wise and surely will be able to find a solution for relieving my boredom. If not, perhaps it is time to replace him with another that is more amiable and less senile.*

"Page the Tortoise Minister," ordered the Dragon King. The attendant lobster guards waved their long spiny antennas and clicked pairs of giant claws to pass on the royal summons for the ancient tortoise.

"How may this humble servant be of service to you, O great king?" said the tortoise, as he stretched his thick wrinkled neck and lowered the point of his curled beak to the pearl decorated floor to pay homage to his master.

"I'm bored. I want you to think of something interesting and entertaining. You have the burning time of one stick of incense to come up with a solution." The Dragon King paused and dropped his voice an octave to emphasize the seriousness of the matter. "If you succeed, I shall allow you to keep your job. Otherwise, turn in your courtier's gauze cap, and exile yourself from my realm." The King nodded his head toward an attendant sea snake, who immediately touched a stick of sandalwood incense to hot lava rock and set it inside a shell lantern.

The tortoise involuntarily contracted his legs and half of his scaly head into the shell, leaving half of a short tail exposed and twitching in consternation. "Would you like to have a royal feast, Your Majesty? You always did like to eat," suggested the ancient sage.

"No, that will not do. We have been feasting nearly every day, for nigh on three months. My jaws ache from the ceaseless chewing. And get your pointy head out from that silly shell; I want to see you when I am talking to you," the Dragon King shouted, which only caused the tortoise to cringe further into his shell.

At length, the tortoise's head slowly emerged from his body armor and turned toward the Dragon King with a hopeful look. "How long has it been since you visited your brothers, the kings of the other three great oceans? Or mayhap you would rather visit some of your cousins, the lords of the aquatic habitats in the dry world above?"

"No, I don't want to visit my brothers nor any other kinsman. All they ever want to do is eat and debate tidbits of boring gossip repeated to them at the last imperial banquet they attended," he replied while grimacing at the thought of his multitude of relations. "Yuck!" he exclaimed with an emphatic swish of the thick, scaly tail, "and all those bratty nephews and nieces. Besides, if I visit one, I would have to visit them all; or else the others would consider themselves slighted. In order to visit them all, I would have to take special care to bring presents of equal value to all relatives of equal rank, so as not to insult any of them. It is just too troublesome. Think of something that is less strenuous to my purse, while more pleasing to the soul."

The tortoise sighed at the latest rejection, then suddenly, in a swift spin that belied his advanced age, the tortoise jumped upright, stood on his hind legs and stuttered excitedly, "Have, have... you visited the world of the mortals lately, my lord? I understand there is now a new Tang Dynasty, which had overthrown the Sui Empire. I have heard that the new emperor is a wise ruler and the capital city of Chang An teems with visitors from all parts of the world, including members of the Jade Emperor's Court."

The Dragon King's bulging, golden eyes gleamed with interest, as he pondered out loud. "Is that so? Now that's a fine thought. Yes, yes! If the gods of the Heaven could be enticed to visit that city, there must be something worthwhile to see. It has been decades since I explored the wonders of the human realm, perhaps the time has come for me to become reacquainted with that part of the world." The King sat up and leaned forward in his throne to address the Tortoise Minister. "Once again your wisdom has proven your worth. You have served me well and shall be properly rewarded." While his words still resonated around the walls of his watery palace, the Dragon King launched himself off the throne and glided toward the exit. The Commander of the lobster guards frantically clicked his claws to summon the royal entourage but, with a flick of his tail, the Dragon King sent a tidal wave of water at the Guard Commander. "Now, stop that silly racket. I don't need an army to protect me in the human world. There is nothing there that can harm me. Just watch the palace until my return." The lobster guards and the Tortoise Minister kept their heads bowed low until the scaly royal tail disappeared from sight.

The King roared in exhilaration as he shot up through the ocean, scattering schools of aquatic creatures in his wake. At the surface of the water, he danced into the air, floating ever higher with the thermal current. The bright noon sun glinted off his scales, reflecting in flashes of blue, green, red and gold bolts of light. He landed on a bed of clouds and commandeered a cluster of the gray-white cumulus to ferry him westward. The King of the Eastern Ocean preferred riding the cloud chariot to flying on his own power, as befitting his social status. Besides, the cloud concealed his body from mortal eyes. It would not be proper for a deity to be seen by mere mortals in his true form.

Soon, the puffy white ball of cumulus hovered over Chang An, the City of Eternal Tranquility and Capital of the Imperial Tang Empire. From his concealed vantage in the sky, the Dragon King spied a vibrant metropolis with broad eight-lane boulevards and crowded streets. The immense size and vitality of the city gave evidence to the power and majesty of the new Imperial Empire. An ornate sprawling palace stood in the center of the city. At the foot of the palace steps tall black pennants lined the borders of the parade ground, with ample room to accommodate all three ten-thousand-men divisions of the imperial guard. A giant walled compound stood near the northeast corner of the parade ground. The sing-song litany of Confucian scholars rose over the walls of the Imperial University, to duel with the steady drones of Buddhist chants that rolled over the roof of the golden-tiled White Horse Temple, situated immediately adjacent to the Imperial school.

The fragrant aroma of cooked food in the marketplace tickled the Dragon King's nose and reminded him that he had not eaten since breakfast. *Why should I remain hungry, when there are so many delicacies below, ready for sampling? But, first, I must make myself presentable to the mortals,* thought the Dragon King. He spun in place three times and said, "Change!" Poof! A spell of disguise cloaked his body. To the average mortal, he now looked like a middle-aged Confucian scholar in a long, blue silk robe with large sweeping sleeves. In place of the original stag-horned dragon-head and the long snout, he sported a small goatee with coiffure hair that was tied in a neatly combed knot atop his head. As a final touch, he opened a collapsible ivory-spine fan to complete the guise. Enshrouded in a cloudy fog, he descended into a side street near the city's marketplace. Once on the ground, he waved away the cloud chariot and walked into the streets of Chang An; no one seemed to have noticed the arrival of a new visitor to the Capital city.

The obvious prosperity of the Tang Empire impressed the Dragon King. It was a drastic contrast from the war and famine plagued land that he remembered from his previous visit over one hundred years ago. Throngs of people from all parts of the world crowded the streets. The general populace appeared well fed and happy, no beggars patrolled street corners for alms. From a market square inside the northeastern gate of the city, crashing gongs announced the performance of an acrobatic troupe. A cacophony of sounds and aromatic scents rose up to assault one's senses. He decided to start his adventure by foraging through the marketplace. A handful of bear's paws went down the gullet with a draught of tiger bone wine; a string of steamed aromatic lotus chestnuts accompanied a fragrant brew of Green Bamboo Silk and satisfied his palate. *Yes, it has been a while since I have sampled such delicacies,* he thought. None of this was available in his watery realm. At length, he emerged from the marketplace burping fumes of the fiery sorghum liquor. He felt as if he was ready to float on air; and he would have too, if he had not, remembered his environment at the last minute.

The Dragon King patted his full belly with contentment and burped a thought. *Now let's find some food for the soul and the spirit*. His wandering eyes locked onto a large crowd near the White Horse Temple, at the edge of the parade ground. The Dragon King jostled his way to the front of the crowd, ignoring the complaints and objections hurled in his direction.

Under the shade of a tall umbrella pine, a fortune teller sat at a wobbly, makeshift table with his back against the temple wall. A broad straw hat half concealed his face as he dispensed fortunes to all comers. Tied to the tree trunk, a short bamboo pole supported a large white pennant with three bold, black words - LIU BAN SHIEN (Liu the Half-God). The man rhythmically shook a tube of bamboo joss stick, and cheerfully raked in coins with the round paper fan he held in his other hand. Between customers he boasted, "All predictions guaranteed. You can smash my sign and have your money back if my prediction does not come to pass."

A slight glow of interest appeared in the golden eyes of the Dragon King as he cleared his throat to draw attention to himself. "Can you foretell the future about everything?"

"Yes, of course," came the immediate response, with neither an upward glance nor a break in the rhythmic shaking of the joss sticks. "As I have previously declared to all the good people here, if my prediction does not hold true, you may have the pleasure of smashing my signs, plus the refund of your fee."

The Dragon King made a show of prolonged deliberation then asked. "How much rain will fall tomorrow at noon," he paused for effect then added smugly, "in this city?" He glowed with self-satisfaction at the looks of surprise and incredulity from the crowd, basking in their admiration for having thought of a tricky question.

In the ensuing silence, Liu stopped rattling his joss sticks and lifted his head to affix a pair of deep-set ebony eyes, half hidden under thicket eyebrows, on the Dragon King. Liu lowered his eyes and flexed his right-hand fingers several times, making a show of using the fingertips to aid in mental calculations. He then stroked his goatee with the edge of his fan before offering in a calm voice, "Three inches only, no more and no less."

The quick and confident response surprised the Dragon King. At a loss for words, he reached his right hand into the wide left sleeve and withdrew a string of coins. The string ran through square holes in the center of the coins, which kept the money together for easy access and portability. Untying the ends of the string, he slid three coins from the rest and tossed them onto the table. "All right, we shall see. Here's your fee. I shall return tomorrow, to check on your prediction."

Miffed by the casual manner with which the fortuneteller had foiled the attempted prank, the Dragon King lost his appetite for further revelry. He walked into an alley and disappeared into a light haze. By the time his cloud chariot reached the Eastern Ocean, the Dragon King had regained his joviality. As he approached the Water Crystal Palace, the King thought over the day's events and chuckled to himself with self-satisfied glee—*What fun I will have tomorrow when I smash that idiot of a fortune teller's sign! That country bumpkin does not know that the amount of daily rainfall is controlled by me, the Dragon King of the Eastern Ocean.* He turned loops and somersaults in the water, spreading tidal waves in all direction, in celebration of the practical joke he had concocted on Liu, the fortuneteller.

As the Dragon King entered the palace, he found the Tortoise Minister waiting by the entrance. The King nodded and motioned for the Tortoise to approach. "Thanks to your wonderful suggestion, I have had a very interesting visit to the human world. You should have been there to see it. I have not had such a good time in eons. You shall have a string of the best pearls from my treasury as a reward for your excellent and faithful service. Now, let me tell you what I saw..."

But the Tortoise Minister surprised the Dragon King by interrupting his recounting of the recent adventure. "Thank you, great King. I am pleased that you enjoyed your excursion. However, during your absence, we received an Imperial visitor from the Jade Emperor of the Heaven. The envoy awaits you in the guest quarter for an audience with you."

Stymied at the relating of his recent escapade, the Dragon King sighed. "Oh well. I have returned, so it is back to work, is it not? All right, bring on the messenger." The Tortoise Minister nodded, and a seahorse quickly darted forth to fetch the Imperial courier.

Just as the Dragon King settled into his throne, a red-faced courtier with a flowing gray beard floated serenely into the palace, his glittering blue robe contrasted brightly against the dim lighting of the ocean bottom. A slight bow of the head served as a salutation from the Imperial envoy to the Dragon King. "I bring you an Imperial edict from the Jade Emperor of the Heaven." So saying, the messenger flicked his right hand to fling back the wide sleeve and produced a rolled up scroll.

In accordance with the Imperial law, the Dragon King rose from his seat, stepped off his dais, walked toward the messenger, and then knelt to accept the scroll. A mere King of the Eastern Ocean must pay proper respect to an edict from the Jade Emperor of the Heaven.

The Dragon King unrolled the scroll and read its content:

'The Dragon King of the Eastern Ocean is hereby directed to let fall three inches of rain on the Tang Capital city of Chang An, at noon of the next day.'

The shocked Dragon King struggled to maintain his composure as he nodded to the courtier and signaled for the secretary crab to affix the royal seal on the document, acknowledging receipt and understanding of the Imperial edict. After the departure of the messenger, the Dragon King lost all interest in recounting his escapade in the mortal realm. With an angry snap of his tail, he dismissed the Tortoise Minister. The ruler of the Eastern Ocean slouched on his throne to ponder in isolation the implications of the recently received Imperial edict.

That evening, the Crystal Palace remained solemnly dark and quiet. No one dared to intrude on the pensive mood of the monarch. The Dragon King retired early, and through the night, palace guards cringed and scampered for cover, as the palace grounds rumbled and shook with roars of frustrated fury that emanated from the royal chamber. The undersea tremors sent tsunamis rippling toward the land, swamping fishing boats and ravaging the coastal villages.

The next day, near noon, a tired and frustrated Dragon King summoned his rainmaking entourage to the ocean surface. The water still boiled in tall waves, remnants of the fury of last night's tempest in the Crystal Palace. The troupe of demigods soared en masse into the air then commandeered a magnificent bed of dark cumulus before soaring to the sky over Chang An. At the exact hour of noon, the Dragon King ordered the beak-nosed Thunder God and Goddess to rattle thunder and lightning over the city. Next, he signaled for the Rain Goddess to ladle measured scoops of rain onto earth. But, instead of three inches of rainfall decreed by the Imperial edict, the Dragon King poured two and a half inches of water onto Chang An. When the rain ceased, the Dragon King ordered the Thunder God to lead the rainmaking troupe back to the Eastern Ocean.

As the group of demigods disappeared over the horizon, the Dragon King resumed the disguise of the previous day and descended onto the streets of Chang An. He hummed a new opera tune that he had learned only the day before, as he strode toward the marketplace with determination. People came out of their rain shelters, and shop owners begin to remove rain flaps from storefronts. Near the White Horse Temple, Liu Ban Shien's stall sat in its usual place, and people had already started to gather at the table. In the excitement of the moment, the Dragon King failed to notice that the area within ten feet of Liu's table remained free of water. He tossed away the remains of a well-gnawed chicken claw and rubbed his hand in glee as he marched to the fore of the crowd. He pounded the table with undisguised enthusiasm, and crowed "Ha! You phony swindler, you were wrong yesterday. You said it would rain three inches today, but we only received two and a half inches from the Heaven. Now, I'm going to smash your sign, to show what a fraud you are."

The Dragon King reached over to grasp the pennant; but, his hand froze on the pennant staff as he heard Liu's voice, through the uproar of the gathered crowd, in a low and somber tone, "I suggest you go home and put your personal affairs in order, little snakeling. What you did at noon today was in direct violation of an Imperial edict, which is a capital offense. As we speak, a detachment of the Guards of the Heaven is on its way to arrest you for incarceration and judgment."

With a spine-chilling shudder, the Dragon King realized the enormity of his misdeed. He sank to his knees and pleaded, "Oh Master Liu, I have just now realized the measure of my follies. You must save me, for you are partially responsible for my predicament."

Liu sighed and nodded in agreement. "True, I am partially responsible for your predicament, thus am obligated to show you a way out. The fact is that the Jade Emperor has already sentenced you to death. You are to be executed three days from today, at the first hour of the afternoon. Wei Cheng has been designated as the presiding magistrate for your execution. You can save yourself by preventing Wei Cheng from officiating at the execution at the specified time. But if you should live beyond the execution hour, then your life shall be spared.

"As you know, Wei Cheng is the First Minister to the Court of Li Shih-Min, the reigning Tang Emperor of the mortal realm. I must warn you, killing Wei Cheng is not the solution. It will only cause another magistrate to be appointed to take his place. Besides, the murder of an Imperial magistrate appointed by the Jade Emperor will only add to your list of misdeeds against the Heavenly Realm. I suggest you seek the Emperor Li Shih-Min's assistance. He may be able to do something for you." Liu then rose from his stool and walked away from the Dragon King, leaving behind his tools of the trade. The Dragon King tried to follow and learn more details from the fortuneteller but no matter how fast he ran, Liu somehow always managed to stay ahead of him. Finally, Liu's body faded into the crowd, and the Dragon King realized that he had just encountered a fellow deity of the Heavenly Realm.

That night, at the hour of the Rat, a misty cloud descended into the Imperial bedchamber in Chang An. A low and persistent voice awakened Li Shih-Min, Emperor of the Tang Empire. He sat up and blinked his eyes to seek the source of the insolent noise. The sight of a man with a dragon's head shocked him into full consciousness. The creature, which wore a golden dragon robe and a royal crown, knelt three feet from his bed. The Tang Emperor found himself gasping for air, as he attempted to summon his attendant eunuchs and guards. Eerily, no one responded to his gasped commands. Through the window, he noticed a heavy gray haze cloaked about the Imperial bedchamber. Left with no other option, Emperor Li turned to face the intruder. The dragon-headed man opened his long, bewhiskered snout, and human words poured forth, "please do not be alarmed, Honored Emperor. I mean you no harm, for I am here to beg for your generous mercy to preserve my own worthless life."

Having recovered slightly from the initial surprise, Li Shih-Min composed himself and restored some regal air to his countenance. "Rise, dragon man. I see from your attire that you, too, are a royal personage. Who are you, and what is it that you wish from me?"

"I'm the Dragon King of the Eastern Ocean. Because I violated an edict of the Jade Emperor of the Heaven, I have been sentenced to be executed three days hence, at the first hour of the afternoon."

Intrigued, the Tang Emperor scratched his chin in puzzlement. "Since the sentence was issued by the Jade Emperor of the Heaven, what can I, although an emperor but still a mere mortal, do to save you? Do you wish that I should go to the Jade Emperor and intercede on your behalf? I did not know the power of a mortal emperor extended upward into the Heavenly realm."

The Dragon King shook his head in response. "I am afraid your authority is limited to the human world. It is, however, within your power to preserve my life from the executioner's knife. You have power over the mortals within your empire, which includes Wei Cheng, your First Minister. The Jade Emperor appointed Minister Wei as the officiating magistrate at my execution. If you would prevent Wei Cheng from attending the execution at the appointed hour, my life will be spared. The Heavenly edict is only valid at that exact hour, by surviving beyond that time I will have gained a reprieve from the Jade Emperor's sentence." The Dragon King remained on his knees and planned to refuse to rise unless the Tang Emperor agreed to save his life.

By this time, Li Shih-Min had lost all fear of the Dragon King. He felt somewhat elated that his First Minister held such an esteemed position in the Heavenly Realm. The opportunity to influence the life and death of a deity boosted the emperor's ego. Besides, it would be nice to have a deity for a friend, especially one so important as the King of the Eastern Ocean. The Tang Emperor felt tempted to test his power within the Jade Emperor's domain. However, true to his reputation as a wise and prudent ruler, Li Shih-Min did not allow pride and ego to overcome his sense of responsible judgment. It would be unwise to incur the wrath of the Jade Emperor. "Tell me specifically, what crime did you commit to earn such a drastic sentence from the Jade Emperor?" The Tang Emperor inquired before committing himself to a decision.

"I am a victim of my own follies;" the Dragon King lowered his stag-horned-head and whimpered in misery. "As ruler of the Eastern Ocean, I control the rainfall in this part of the mortal world. The day before yesterday, I toured Chang An in disguise. While doing so, a fortuneteller tricked me into a bet. The man predicted that three inches of rain would fall from the sky during the next day. You can imagine my surprise when I went home and found an edict from the Jade Emperor, ordering me to let fall exactly three inches of rain in the city of Chang An. So, yesterday, I came over your city and created your mid-day thunderstorm. But instead of the three inches of water as decreed by the Jade Emperor, I allowed only two and a half inches to fall to the ground. For that, I am to be executed."

Emperor Li Shih-Min pondered over the Dragon King's tale; *the punishment does appear to be too extreme for such a minor infraction.* He nodded his head as he came to a decision. "That is indeed too harsh a penalty for shorting half an inch of rain. I shall keep Wei Cheng from officiating at your appointment with the executioner. Of course, you do realize my people need the rain for their crops." The Dragon King bobbed his snout and kowtowed in gratitude before he retreated into the gray haze, which dissipated into nothingness.

The Tang Emperor thought it had been nothing but a dream, but he found himself still sitting at the edge of the bed as if he had actually been talking to someone. Again, he attempted to summon the attendant eunuch and guards. This time they responded almost immediately, but they trembled and prostrated in fear at hearing that an individual had entered the Imperial bedchamber without their knowledge.

Puzzled and intrigued by the vividness of the strange dream, Li Shih-Min dismissed the guards and sent a eunuch to summon the court astrologer. The old sage arrived barefooted and stood attentively while the emperor related his encounter with the Dragon King. "Normally, I would advise Your Majesty against meddling into the affairs of the Heaven. But since Your Majesty has already promised to save the Dragon King's life, it is best to carry it out. Otherwise, if the Dragon King dies, his soul may come back to haunt your dragon personage."

"But it was only a dream, was it not? And how do I go about preventing the execution?"

"It could have been just a dream, but considering the vividness of your description, I recommend against discounting its validity. I suggest Your Majesty summon Wei Cheng on that fateful day and keep him by your Imperial person the entire afternoon. This way, Wei Cheng will not be able to officiate at the Dragon King's execution." Unable to think of a better solution, Li Shih-Min nodded his head and dismissed the Court Astrologer.

Early in the morning, on the appointed day of the Dragon King's execution, the Tang Emperor summoned Wei Cheng for a private audience regarding affairs of the Empire. He then kept Wei Cheng with him through the noon repast, followed by a walk through the Imperial garden, to inspect damages caused by the thunderstorm of three days before. As the first hour of the afternoon neared, the emperor noticed that Wei Cheng appeared to be preoccupied. The esteemed First Minister, usually eloquent with prose, was having a hard time maintaining a coherent conversation. At the third failed attempt to complete a train of thought, Wei Cheng complained of tiredness and requested to be excused from the emperor's presence. This very much alarmed Li Shih-Min, who shook his head in adamant refusal. "If you are tired, we shall rest here, in the garden pavilion. Perhaps a game of Wei-Qi will relax the tension from your body. Besides, I wish to hone my skills at the game and you are the best player available." The much-distressed First Minister reluctantly bowed his submission.

Several times during the game, Wei Cheng fidgeted in discomfort and reiterated his supplication to be excused; each time, Li Shih-Min stubbornly refused to change his decision. Wei Cheng, unable to concentrate on the game, quickly lost the first match. The Tang Emperor immediately insisted on another game, and again denied Wei Cheng's appeal to withdraw from the palace. At the exact moment of the first hour of the afternoon, Wei Cheng nodded off and fell asleep on the round marble game table. Li Shih-Min breathed a sigh of relief and gazed guiltily at his First Minister for keeping the man from his appointed duty to the Jade Emperor of the Heaven. *I suppose that's one way to keep him from his appointment. Besides, a sleeping man could not possibly officiate at an execution.* The emperor rose from the white marble stool and quietly walked over to gently cover Wei Cheng with the golden Imperial robe to protect the First Minister from the cool breeze in the garden.

After an incense's burning time beyond the first hour of the afternoon, Wei Cheng jerked awake from his slumber, sopping with sweat. He shook his head, wiped his brow with a broad sleeve then sighed aloud, "what a tiring business!"

Surprised, then puzzled, and finally alarmed by Wei Cheng's peculiar comment, Li Shih-Min quickly demanded an explanation. "Why were you tired? All you did was fall asleep during our game of Wei-chi."

Wei Cheng snapped his head about, as if he had just noticed the presence of his emperor for the first time, then hurriedly stood up and adjusted his courtier's gauze cap before making his bow. "A thousand apologies for this unworthy one's unconscionable behavior in your Imperial presence, Master. I don't know what came over ..."

The emperor impatiently waved him into silence. "Never mind that. Tell me about the business which has so tired you."

Wei Cheng paused to gather his thoughts and shook his head again in bewilderment. "Master, please do not think me insane, but, I had a most incredible dream. It seemed that I was sent for by the Jade Emperor of the Heaven to officiate at the execution of a prisoner. It was an eerie experience. There I sat at the officiating magistrate's table, while a man with a dragon's head and a human body knelt in front of me. He appeared to be a member of the royalty, as evidenced by the golden dragon robe on his person. I read the charges, verified the execution order and the identity of the prisoner - who turned out to be the Dragon King of the Eastern Ocean. Finally, I gave the order to chop off the prisoner's head."

In shock, Emperor Li Shih-Min realized that while Wei Cheng's body had been in the Imperial garden, his spirit had gone and carried out the execution order. Before he could recover from Wei Cheng's eerie tale, their attentions were drawn toward a commotion among the Imperial entourage who had been waiting patiently outside of the pavilion. A distraught Commander of the Imperial Guard approached the emperor and knelt to report that the bloody head of a dragon had fallen from the sky onto the Imperial parade ground in front of the palace—the execution ground of condemned criminals. Li Shih-Min and Wei Cheng turned to look at each other in stunned silence.

That night, a strange swirling wind hung over the Imperial Palace. Shrill howls haunted the halls of the buildings. In the Imperial bedchamber, the Tang Emperor dreamed of being chased by a headless man wearing a golden dragon robe. Words gurgled forth from the neatly severed and bloody neck to haunt the emperor, "Give me back my head! Give me back my head!" Li Shih-Min awakened, bathed in sweat, and immediately summoned the Court Astrologer.

Again, the bearded old courtier stumbled in with bared feet and a rumpled robe to listen to the recounting of the nightmare. The Astrologer paced the floor, while sagely nodding his head as the emperor sat anxiously for his interpretation of the dream. "It would appear that the soul of the Dragon King blamed Your Majesty for his death, which was the reason he haunted the palace." He took care to avoid any hint of gloating over his previous admonition regarding meddling in Heavenly affairs. "As for how to get rid of the haunting spirit, I recommend a rite of protection prayers to the gods."

In the ensuing days, battalions of Daoist priests in long flowing blue robes invaded the palace. They waved long swords bedecked with rune-inscribed strips of yellow paper and chanted spells. Larger and longer versions of the yellow paper decorated each wall and doorway in the palace, with an especially heavy treatment in and around the Imperial bedchamber. Their efforts only succeeded in keeping the rest of the palace awake.

As for the emperor, his nightmare continued unabated. Changing his bedroom confused only the serving eunuchs, not the ghost. At the suggestion of the Court Astrologer, throngs of Buddhist monks wearing red and gold robes replaced the Daoist priests. During all hours of the day and night, the fragrant aroma of smoking sandalwood incense, the chiming of bells and the chants of spiritual purification permeated the palace. All agreed that the soothing Buddhist chants were infinitely more bearable than the shouted Daoist spells. However, the headless ghost of the Dragon King continued to terrorize the Imperial personage. At times, flying pieces of roof tile rained down upon unsuspecting residents of the palace.

The lack of rest quickly reduced the Tang Emperor to a haggard wreck, and his rapidly deteriorating health alarmed the Imperial Court. The story of the emperor and his headless ghost had initially been the subject of many a witty tale in the palace. Now, with the emperor's life threatened, it was no longer a laughing matter. The Empire had only recently been united after a long and drawn out civil war. A struggle for succession to the throne could easily bring about another decade of bloody conflict. Li Shih-Min had been a benevolent and able ruler. The Empire could not afford to lose him at the prime of his life. In desperation, the emperor's two favorite generals—Wei-Tse Kung and Chin Shu-Bao—volunteered to personally guard the emperor against the spirit of the Dragon King. The two generals were famous for their valiant prowess in battle. General Wei-Tse held the honor of First General of the Realm, the military counterpart to the First Minister Wei Cheng.

That night, the two generals commenced patrolling the emperor's bedchamber. Surprisingly, for the first time since the demise of the Dragon King, Li Shih-Min had a restful sleep. During the next seven nights, Wei-Tse Kung and Chin Shu-Bao continued guarding the Imperial bedchamber and succeeded in keeping the ghost at bay.

As the two generals were of flesh and blood, they could not be expected to guard the emperor every night, forever. An alternative solution was required. At the suggestion of Wei Cheng, court artists painted full-sized portraits of the two generals, resplendent in full armor and weaponry. The paintings were then mounted at the entrances and windows of the Imperial bedchamber. To the joy and relief of everyone, the portraits also kept the Dragon King's spirit away, thus relieving the two generals from their nightly duties.

Intrigued by the unexpected success of the two generals, the Court Astrologer remembered the story about the Dragon King's encounter with Liu the fortuneteller. The Court Astrologer obtained the eight characters of the two generals, which provided their date and time of birth, and took them to the marketplace. Under a tall umbrella pine near the White Horse Temple, he found Liu Ban Shien, just as had been described by the Dragon King. Handing over three coins, along with the two portraits and the eight characters, he posed his question, "tell me, Sir, can these two individuals ward off evil demons?" Liu read the eight characters before glanced over the portraits.

"Yes, they can protect one from ghosts and spirits. In their previous lives, they were the Jade Emperor's Personal Guards. For the misdeed of a drunken brawl at an Imperial banquet, they were sentenced to reincarnate into the human world. Their penance was to aid Li Shih-Min in his great venture of uniting China. At the end of this cycle of their lives, they shall return to their previous positions in the Heaven."

News of the two generals' ability to ward off evil spirits quickly passed from the Imperial palace to the populace. From that time onward, the two generals became guardians of Chinese households, and were known as the "Door Gods." Their portraits have since been preserved for eternity, gracing doorways of Chinese households to ward off evil spirits. The red-faced general is Chin Shu-Bao, while the black-faced general is Wei Tse-Gung. They are especially prominent during the time of the Chinese New Year.

Over one hundred years later, An Lu-Shan, a Tartar chieftain allied to the realm, rose in rank to become a general of the Imperial Tang Empire. He rebelled against Emperor Tang Ming-Huang, a great-grandson of Li Shih-Min. The rebel army sacked Chang An before it was finally vanquished by the loyalist General Ko Tse-Ie.

Some people believed An Lu-Shan was the Dragon King reincarnated, bent on revenge against descendants of Li Shih-Min; while General Ko was the fortuneteller Liu Ban-Shien, sent by the Jade Emperor to save the Tang Empire.

7
THE OLD MAN UNDER THE MOON

Amongst the multitude of deities of Chinese mythology, one very popular figure is known by the unusual title of "The Old Man Under the Moon." This appellation originates from the legend that he is most frequently seen at night annotating his marriage register under a bright moonlit sky. To this date, a matchmaker is often referred to as The Old Man Under the Moon.

Wei Ku came from a prominent aristocratic family in Bin Chou. Everyone expected him to gain an exalted post in the service of the emperor via the national examination system, the time-honored path to prominence.

On his twentieth spring, a very excited but confident Wei Ku set off to participate in the biannual national civil service examination at Chang An, the Capital City of the Imperial Tang Empire. Wei Lai-Fu, a household guard accompanied him as servant and bodyguard. Several times during the first few hours of the trip, Lai Fu had to remind the young master to slow down. The servant could not keep up with the eager pace set by the young master, who was not burdened by the weight of all the clothing, books and other necessities for the sojourn.

Two days later, they entered Sung-Cheng, a very convenient halfway point city en route to the Capital. The sun had exhausted most of its strength and was about to rest behind the western hills when Wei Ku led the way through the city gate. He easily found Lai An Chu-Inn of Peaceful Rest-the hostel mentioned by his father as the most suitable establishment in the city. The elder Wei had stayed at the same hostel twenty years ago, when he, too, had traveled to take his national civil service examination. As a matter of fact, the grandfather of Wei Ku had used the same rest stop when he took it. The establishment offered clean facilities, served good food, was void of bedbugs, and did not cater to boisterous clientele; an ideal environment for a scholar preparing for his examination.

Leaving Lai-Fu to unpack, the young scholar passed through the beaded curtain at the entryway and strolled toward the outskirts of the city, hoping for a cool evening breeze by the riverbank. Soon, a slightly embarrassed Wei Ku found himself lost in the unfamiliar city. His searching eyes noticed an old man standing at a secluded corner of the market square. Tilting his head to accommodate the moonlight, the elderly gentleman leaned on a tall gnarled staff as he leafed through a well-worn tome. Wei Ku thought *it must have been a famous classic for a man to be so engrossed as to read it by the moonlight.* He eagerly walked over and bowed respectfully as was the proper behavior for a Confucian scholar greeting an elderly gentleman. "Excuse me, learned master. May I ask what interesting volume you are reading?" A very appropriate and polite opening to get acquainted before seeking assistance and direction.

The old man waved a hand, shooing away some gnats buzzing between his eyes and the book, as he replied without looking up from his reading. "This is the Official Marriage Register of the Heaven. It is my responsibility to arrange marriages. This book records all past, present and future marriages under the Heaven."

The intended quest for directions died on Wei Ku's lips. He stammered as he wondered whether the old man was insane or making a jest at a stranger's expense. As he wavered between vexation and curiosity, the old man lifted his head, revealing a set of shiny golden eyes, framed in long, drooping, snow-white eyebrows with deeply wrinkled sockets. He chuckled, "You don't believe me, do you, young man?" Slightly embarrassed by the old man's blunt perceptiveness, Wei Ku smiled hesitantly and sheepishly nodded his agreement with the statement. "You see that sack at my feet?" the old man continued while pointing with his long staff, "It holds red sashes that I use to bind couples together as husbands and wives." Wei Ku's eyes followed the man's gesturing hand. Sure enough, partially hidden by Wei Ku's shadow, beside the old man's feet, lay a lumpy cloth sack. Through the half-open mouth of the sack, Wei Ku saw bundled lengths of bright red silk ribbons.

Wei Ku did not know what to make of the old man's regal demeanor and the confident tone regarding his professed profession. *Well, why not humor him. If nothing else, he could at least help me find my way back to the hostel. Besides, he does seem to fit the description of the legendary Old Man Under the Moon.* Intrigued by the thought of his knowing the identity of his own potential mate, Wei Ku asked hopefully, "Do you mean you can tell me who is to share my life to the days when my hair turned gray and white?"

The old man raised his eyebrows and squinted in a knowing smile while nodding his silver locks fringed dome in acknowledgment. "Most certainly young man; all I need is your name, hometown, and family origin."

"I'm Wei Ku, son of Lord Wei Yuen-Chang, Governor of the city of Bin Chou and great-grandson of Wei Cheng, the Prime Minister to Emperor Tai Chung, and the great-grandfather of our Imperial master." Eagerly responded the young scholar.

Wei Ku was slightly disappointed that the old man did not appear suitably impressed by the august Wei lineage, nor by the elder Wei's exalted position. The old man casually thumbed his tongue for saliva and quickly flipped through the dog-eared pages of the tome. "Let's see, Wei Ku of Bin Chou. Ah, I see that your future bride-to-be lives right here in this city. Do you wish to see what she looks like?"

Surprised at the quick response and the unexpected offer, Wei Ku was again at a loss for words. What an unusual opportunity. Most people meet their mates for the first time on their nuptial eve. Traditionally, only the matchmaker and the parents knew what the young bride and groom looked like before the wedding. At that thought, Wei Ku lost all sense of composure and his head bobbed eagerly, like a hungry chick pecking at grains of rice. "Yes, yes, old master, yes! And I shall be forever grateful."

"Well, come on then, young man." The old man shoved the big book inside the sack, drew it shut then slung it over the left shoulder. Lifting his crooked staff to lead the way, he set off at a brisk pace toward the heart of the city. The old man traversed small twisting side streets as if he grew up in the city. Finally, he slowed as they approached what appeared to be the center of the city, with a marketplace and a city square. They stopped at a corner near the edge of the marketplace. "There is your future bride," said the old man, as he pointed at a young woman setting up a vegetable stand for the next morning's business.

The very idea of a marriage between the scion of an Imperial Prime Minister and a lowly peasant enraged Wei Ku. He struggled with his composure, and it was a while before he could trust himself to speak. "You can't, you can't...er.. expect me to marry that,...that person. I'm of a respected noble family. You cannot possibly mean that I am to be matched with a mere peasant wench. Besides, she seems to be in her late teens, a little too old to be my match."

The old man chuckled at the indignation of the youth. "No, no, you are mistaken. Your wife is not the vegetable vendor. She is the mother of your bride-to-be. Your match is that little girl seated beside her."

Wei Ku took a few steps forward for a closer look. Sure enough, half hidden within the shadows, a little girl sat on a small stool playing in the muddy ground beside the vegetable vendor. Despite the bright moonlight, Wei Ku could see little more than the barest outline of the little girl. However, he had no trouble noting the frayed and heavily patched clothing worn by the mother. The longer he looked, the angrier he became. Wei Ku raged at the thought that an old man would play such a crass joke on a stranger. But, when the young scholar turned around, the old sage had disappeared. Wei Ku ran down the side streets and searched through the market area. But the old rascal had vanished. Finally, tired and soaked with sweat, a very frustrated Wei Ku hired an urchin to lead him back to the hostel. Along the way, he thought about the old man's prediction and became increasingly agitated. By the time he arrived at the hostel, Wei Ku had worked himself into a rage.

The thought of marrying a common peasant's daughter continued to trouble him through the night, and the lack of sleep did not improve his disposition. *It was probably a prank,* he thought, but the legend of the 'Old Man Under the Moon' was too well known to be discounted. *I must do something to save myself from marrying a peasant girl.* Before dawn, Wei Ku roused Lai-Fu out of his cot in the courtyard and whispered through gritted teeth. "Go to the marketplace and kill that girl!"

The sleepy servant jerked into full alertness. "What girl, young master? And why do you want me to kill her?" Came the hesitant reply from the frightened and befuddled servant.

"Keep quiet, and just do as you are told. I want you to go to the public market and look for a young female vegetable vendor. She runs a stall at the northern edge of the market. The woman has a young daughter of about two years old with her. The person I want you to kill is the daughter."

Lai-Fu was fearful but had no choice but to obey the order of his master. To refuse would result in a beating, plus the loss of livelihood. The servant searched through the travel luggage, but the only item that could be used as a weapon was a pair of scissors. He hid the scissors inside the wide sleeve of his jacket and stumbled out of the hostel to do his master's bidding.

Lai-Fu easily found the little girl at the vegetable stand in the marketplace, just as described by Wei Ku. The little girl sat behind the stall of vegetables, in the protective arms of her mother, and out of Lai-Fu's reach. He paced the area, seeking a way to get near the intended victim. With the approaching dawn, the market began to fill with people. In desperation, the servant took the scissors from his sleeve and threw it at the little girl. The scissors flew true and hit the child on the head. Blood spurted from the wound as she slid through her mother's arm to the ground without a whimper. The horrified mother screamed and dove under the stall to rescue her daughter. In the ensuing chaos, Lai-Fu made good his escape. Even though he did not actually see the little girl die, he reported as having accomplished the assigned task.

The incident gnawed at Wei Ku's mind for the remainder of the trip. He was pensive, despondent and irritable. After taking the civil service examination, Wei Ku did not remain at the Imperial capital to take in the sights as previously planned, nor did he visit his father's colleagues as was proper. Instead, he headed straight home–bypassing Sung Cheng–to await the Imperial proclamation of the results of the examination. This time, however, there would be no published list of top-ranked candidates for exulted positions at the Imperial Court. Within ten days of Wei Ku's return home, a rebellion had broken out on the northwestern frontier. An Lu-San, a Tartar Commander in a western province of the Tang Empire, decided to make himself the new emperor. The realm had enjoyed thirty odd years of tranquility under the benevolent rule of Emperor Tang Ming-Huang. The people prospered, while the army deteriorated in war readiness due to complacency and neglect. Within one month, the rebels routed the Imperial Army and sacked the Capital, forcing the Tang Emperor to flee south.

News of the An Lu San rebellion quickly spread to all parts of the realm, including Bin Chou. Suddenly, everyone in the Wei mansion focused his attention on the rebellion. Governor Wei Yuen-Chang ordered immediate mobilization of the provincial militia. Wei Ku welcomed the distraction offered by the insurrection. The threat against the Imperial realm provided an easy escape from his sense of guilt. Besides, sacrificing himself on the battlefield would be an honorable way to atone for his misdeed. He refused to become an officer in his father's army. Instead, Wei Ku enlisted in the loyalist force in the neighboring province as a common soldier.

Wei Ku fought bravely in countless campaigns against rebel forces. The martial lessons from Wei Lai-Fu bore fruit. His superiors recognized the courage, martial skill and leadership abilities of the young man, and Wei Ku quickly rose to the rank of an officer.

One day, Wei Ku found himself summoned to join the Commanding General and his staff at the head table of a victory celebration. General Wang Hsing seemed to be exceptionally friendly toward Wei Ku, praised him profusely for his martial ability and valor. Halfway through the meal, the General leaned over and said, "Tell me about your family background. You have been in my service for fifteen years. If my mind and eyes are not too dull, I am convinced you are of noble lineage."

Puzzled at the Commander's sudden interest in his genealogy, Wei Ku pondered his words carefully before making his response. "Sir, I am from the family of Lord Wei Yuen-Chang of Bin Chou."

"Aha, I was right. You are from a noble family. I commend you for your dedication to the emperor. In the past 15 years, I do not recall you ever taking leave to visit your family. Have you been communicating with them?"

"Sir, my father is also in the field in my home province and my mother is at home in Bin Chou. Thank you for your concern, they are both healthy and well."

"What about your wife and children?"

A slightly embarrassed Wei Ku hesitated before answering, "Although I am thirty-five years old, I am still single."

"How is it that you, being a member of such a prestigious family, are still unwed?"

"Sir, I had hoped to be a government official, thus until the age of 20, I devoted myself to studies of the Confucian classics. I had just taken the national civil service examination when the bandit An Lu-Shan started this rebellion. Rather than wait for the opportunity to come to me, I decided to reach out and grab it. In times of turmoil, a soldier is more valuable than a scholar. Besides, I wanted to stop the bandits before they destroy my family. That was fifteen years ago. For the moment, the army is my home. Until this rebellion is quelled, no man and especially no soldier should consider having a family." At that, Wei Ku self-consciously picked up his wine cup and toasted the General.

The General sipped the drink and responded, "Well said, well said, young man. These are very gallant and honorable thoughts, as it should be for a patriotic young man of good breeding." Impressed with Wei Ku's conviction and loyalty, not to mention his eloquent prose, the General nodded his head and stroked his beard, then added, "It is rare indeed to have such fine poet and soldier embodied in one person. I propose a union to cement the bond between our two families. What do you say?"

Surprised at the suddenness of the proposal from the General, Wei Ku was at a loss for words. Before he could come up with a proper response, the General continued, "Besides, as a scholar, you should know the Confucian philosophy very well. What did Confucius say was the most serious of the three major sins for a son to commit?"

"No heirs," Wei Ku croaked in a meek voice.

"That's right. Therefore, if you should marry my daughter, you shall have taken the first step toward fulfilling your filial obligations and, at the same time, continue to provide loyal service to the emperor."

With trepidation, Wei Ku rose from his seat and bowed to his Commander. "Thank you for honoring me with the hand of your daughter. I shall immediately write and inform my parents of the joining of our two families."

The General smiled and hiccupped. "I had hoped you would agree to the marriage proposal. My daughter is very young. Please be patient and understanding with her. Here is a set of gold brooches belonging to my family to seal the betrothal." He reached into his robe and brought forth a red bejeweled silk pouch. Untying the silk drawstring, two stunning gold bracelets tumbled into Wei Ku's waiting palms. The blue and red gems decorated the beautifully worked brooches - a matched pair of dragon and phoenix.

Wei Ku carefully returned the brooches to the silk pouch then reached inside his own shirt to bring forth a deep green jade pendant, carved in the image of the Holy Buddha. He presented the pendant to the General. "This is a family heirloom my mother gave me before I left home to join the army. I have protected it with my life and now I entrust it to your daughter, my bride to be."

Well pleased with the exchange of gifts, General Wang Hsing staggered to his feet, which brought the feasting officers to an immediate silence. "We have two good reasons to celebrate today." He paused for effect, "Our great victory against the bandit forces and the betrothal of my daughter to Commander Wei Ku. I hereby declare tomorrow as a day of rest." The entire camp shook with roars of approval. The officers' corps took turns approaching the General's table toasting to the union.

The next day, Wei Ku struggled and finally forced his eyes open to get a glance at his tormentor, only to find his aide shaking his shoulder. Wei Ku groaned and belched into the familiar face, and the rising stench forced the soldier into a stumbling retreat out of the tent. The odor of stale alcohol assaulted Wei Ku's nostrils and succeeded in bringing back memories of the previous evening's events. With another groan, Wei Ku rolled off his cot and staggered out of the tent to get some water. Blinking his eyes in the glaring daylight, he noticed the General's scribe standing by his side. Wei Ku attempted a greeting through his raspy throat, which turned into a painful grunt, and the scribe bowed his respects in return. "General Wang sent me to obtain the 'Eight Characters' of your birth. I am to take them and those of the young mistress to the local fortune teller." Wei Ku nodded in understanding and, in between dry heaves, uttered his Eight Characters—the year, month, day, and hour pillars of his birth on the solar calendar—and supposedly denoted the fortune of the person's life. The scribe bowed again, then hurried to escape the odor surrounding Wei Ku and his tent.

On the third day of the following month, the Provincial Governor—a son of the reigning Tang Emperor—arrived to honor and personally officiate at the wedding ceremony. Amidst blaring trumpets, crashing gongs, beating drums, and exploding firecrackers, the newlywed couple entered the nuptial suite. Once alone, Wei Ku apprehensively lifted the veil and stared into a beautiful oval face, with smooth skin, and a pair of talkative eyes. She appeared to be little more than seventeen years old, slightly old for a maiden to be entering into a marriage. However, the young woman appeared to be intelligent and more than pleasing to the eyes. *I just hope she behaves like a proper wife, instead of a General's daughter,* thought Wei Ku as he turned to pinch out the candles.

In the morning, Wei Ku reclined in bed as he savored the view of his new bride arranging her makeup. He noticed her placing a beauty mole on the center of her forehead. Intrigued by the unusual habit, Wei Ku rose on one elbow and asked, "Why do you wear that beauty mole? You certainly do not need it to enhance your looks."

The young bride glanced timidly at her husband through the reflection in the brass mirror and smiled shyly, "The beauty mole is to cover a scar on my forehead." Then her thin line of dark eyebrows arched, and her face flushed in anger, "Fifteen years ago, a crazy wild man threw a pair of scissors at me, while I sat in my mother's lap. Luckily, the scissors only broke the flesh on my forehead. I was knocked unconscious and ended up with this scar. They never caught the bandit who threw the scissors." Wei Ku's face froze in shocked surprise, while her voice softened to a tender tone as she continued, "I remember the time well. It had been just prior to the beginning of the rebellion. I was only a little over two years old. My parents died trying to flee from the rebels. Fortunately, the General happened to pass by the area and adopted me." She then paused in apprehension as she caught the look of Wei Ku in her mirror, "Are you alright, my honored husband?"

Wei Ku smiled weakly as he recalled the encounter fifteen years ago, with the Old Man Under the Moon.

That which is preordained by the gods shall not be undone by mere mortals.

8

THE COWBOY AND THE SEAMSTRESS

According to Chinese legend, the Milky Way was created by the Jade Emperor to serve as a barrier between two lovers. On the seventh of July of each year flocks of magpies gather to form a bridge spanning the Milky Way so that the estranged couple may join together for that one day.

In the beginning of time the Ox was not the draft animal he is today, used by farmers to till the land. Instead, he lived a comfortable and leisurely life in Heaven with endless fields of green grass and streams of sweet water. But one day the Jade Emperor surveyed the needs of mortals and decided they required help in tilling the land. The giant Ox was powerful and gentle, just the right being for the job.

The Ox, however, was a deity, and thus could not be banished without cause to serve mortals. He had to be induced into volunteering his services. This, of course, would require a great deal of persuasion, along with enticements and, perhaps, some subtle pressure to prod him onto the right path.

The Jade Emperor summoned the Ox to his court. "Have you ever thought about going to live among the mortals of the human world? They have blue skies, green grass, and sweet clear water."

Uncertain at the sudden honor bestowed upon him by the Jade Emperor, the Ox swished his tail and studied the Heavenly Monarch with large, apprehensive eyes. "No, master of all gods, I have never had such thoughts. But, might I inquire as to why do you ask such a question of me?"

Noting the suspicion in the Ox, the Jade Emperor quickly smiled and shrugged nonchalantly in reply. "Oh, I just thought you might enjoy living in the human world, and how happy the mortals would be to have you with them. The humans would love, respect and worship you. They may even build temples to honor you, taking care of your every need." The Ox twitched his ears and stared doubtfully at the Jade Emperor.

The prolonged silence from the Ox compelled the Jade Emperor to launch a new line of persuasion. "You are so grand in size, so powerful in strength and so august in stature, there is nothing like you among the mortals. You would be revered for your strength and good looks. All you need to do is demonstrate your ability to help them work the land and they will cherish and adore you as their savior." The flattery temptingly inflated the bovine ego, but the Ox was still not convinced; his cautious temperament warned against rash decisions. In desperation, the Jade Emperor pressed on. "Listen to me, honored Ox, one should go places and experience things. I say this to you because I think one can be bored with the mundane daily routines here and should be interested in gaining some fame for posterity. If I should lie to you, may my daughter be wed to a mere mortal below us."

The Ox was acquainted with the Jade Emperor's seven daughters, especially the youngest one. She was the prettiest, most skilled seamstress in Heaven, and the favorite daughter of the Heavenly Ruler. The girls often played together in the grassy meadows. The Ox felt that the Jade Emperor would not allow any misfortune to befall any of his daughters. Besides, it would be impolite to refuse a suggestion from the Jade Emperor. *Perhaps the Jade Emperor is upset at me for eating that patch of orchids in the palace garden and wants me out of the way for a while.* With some misgivings, the Ox agreed to go and live among the mortals.

After bidding farewell to his friends, the Ox rode the rainbow down to the mortal realm and quickly realized that the Jade Emperor had not been truthful with him. The grass was often brown and dry, the water was at times muddy, and the sky was not always blue and clear. However, once he had agreed to live among the mortals, he could not return to Heaven without a summons from the Jade Emperor. The Ox decided to bide his time and plot his revenge against the sly ruler of the Heaven.

First, he found a kind young man to care for him. The young man was very poor and his parents had long ago passed away. He lived with his older brother's family. The Ox became the young man's closest friend and in time, for his association with the Ox, the young man became known as the Cowboy. They were very much alike in temperament, both being strong, yet kind and gentle.

Soon after the Ox's entry into the household, he invoked the jealousy of the Cowboy's sister-in-law. She wanted the big Ox for herself but since she could not have him, she nagged her husband into evicting the younger brother from the house. The older brother finally gave in and summoned the Cowboy. "You are now of age and should go forth and seek your own fortune."

"But where should I go? I have lived here all my life."

The older brother looked toward his wife, who glared back and tapped her foot impatiently. In the end, the older brother sighed and said, "I have no idea, but this house is mine by right of inheritance and we have no room for you and that monster of yours."

The Cowboy had no choice but to take the Ox and leave the home of his birth. He bundled his clothing, loaded a cart with his farming tools, and started toward the distant mountain, with the Ox pulling the cart behind him. At the foot of the mountain, the Cowboy built a straw hut for shelter. The Ox helped clear the land for planting crops. The Cowboy worked hard every day and was able to eke out a living. But, except for the Ox, he had no one to talk to, so he was very lonely. He thought about marriage, but who in his right mind would allow a daughter to marry an almost penniless farmer? In his moments of melancholy, the Cowboy poured out his sorrow to his giant companion.

The Ox recalled the promise made by the Jade Emperor and devised a solution that would help his friend and at the same time take revenge against the Jade Emperor. The Ox ambled over and lay down next to the man. "Cowboy, you have been most kind to me and I thank you very much."

"What!" The Cowboy's mouth fell open in shock, as he turned to stare wild-eyed at the Ox, who for the first time, had begun to speak to him in the human language.

The Ox ignored the Cowboy's surprised look and continued calmly. "You must be very lonely having only me for company. You are now full grown and have a good rice field. It is time to find yourself a wife..."

"Find my...myself a wife! Who...er..who would be willing to...to...," stuttered, the surprised Cowboy. He was amazed and embarrassed at learning he had revealed his innermost thoughts to a talking Ox.

"Not to worry, I have a solution."

Now, thought the Cowboy, *this is too much. Not only does he speak, he claims to be able to find a wife for me.* "Solution, what solution? What... what are you talking about?" asked the extremely agitated Cowboy.

The Ox leaned over and licked beads of sweat from the Cowboy's brow. He savored the salty taste and then continued in a smooth and even voice. "Now calm down and listen to me. I did not always live on this land with mortals. I used to live in the Heaven and was tricked by the Jade Emperor into coming down to live among the mortals. He said that if he lied to me, his daughter would wed a mortal. With your help, I shall make his vow come true."

By then the Cowboy had regained some of his composure and became intrigued by the tale. He eagerly nodded his head for the Ox to continue.

"Tomorrow," said the Ox, "you will go to the river that flows on the other side of the mountain. We went there the previous summers, remember?"

The Cowboy again bobbed his head as he recalled the winding silvery river.

"That river is called the Milky Way. It is very clean and clear. You don't know it, but that's the river in which you will find seven young goddesses bathing every summer night. They always undress near the bushes by the river bank, at the same place in the river from which we rested and drank its water. What you must do is steal one of their dresses. The owner of the dress will become your wife."

"But who are these goddesses?"

The Ox winked one of his big brown eyes at the Cowboy, and the long pink tongue flicked out to lick some flies away from his wide snout. "They are the Jade Emperor's seven daughters. Very beautiful ladies all, and excellent seamstresses. They are the ones who sew the rainbows you see in the sky. The youngest daughter is also the prettiest and the best seamstress. They work during the day, then rest and bathe in the evenings."

The Cowboy was skeptical and apprehensive. But the calm, matter-of-fact, demeanor of the Ox convinced the young man. Since the Ox could talk, the whole story might be true.

The next day, the Cowboy left early for the Milky Way and hid in the thick reeds near the river bend as specified by the Ox. Before long, the sun settled behind the distant mountains on the horizon and the golden moon rose into the starry sky. The Cowboy waited patiently and soon was rewarded with magical singing voices drifting down from the Heaven. The voices drew near, and the Cowboy saw seven shiny stars glittering and dancing in the moonlight. Each star was of a different color - red, white, green, yellow, blue, purple and the last, that of a multicolored rainbow. They floated toward the Milky Way and, upon touching the sandy shore of the river, transformed into seven beautiful women. Each was clad in a gown of the color that they had worn as a star. The last star took the shape of a young maiden wearing a seven-colored gown.

The playful way that the other goddesses teased the young maiden pointed to her being the youngest daughter of the Jade Emperor, spoken of by the Ox. As a group, they pranced over to the water's edge. One by one, they slipped out of their clothing and waded into the river to frolic in the cool refreshing water. They sang and splashed each other, washing off the sweat of the day's work.

The Cowboy kept his eyes on the place where the youngest goddess placed her dress. He waited until the goddesses were well into their games and then ran out to scoop up the colorful garment. With dress in hand, he shouted in glee then charged off to hide in the bushes again.

The Cowboy's appearance and his shouts startled the goddesses. But modesty forced them to remain hidden in the water until the intruder had disappeared. When the Cowboy did not return, they rushed ashore to put on their clothing and darted back into the Heaven. But the youngest goddess had nothing to wear, so was unable to fly off with her sisters.

The Cowboy waited until the other goddesses were gone, then came out of his hiding place. The reappearance of the Cowboy forced the young goddess to seek the cover of the river. The Cowboy walked to the edge of the water and offered her dress. "Please marry me. If you agree, I will return your clothing to you." Left with no choice, the young goddess nodded her consent.

When they returned together to the Cowboy's straw hut, the Ox greeted them at the door. The goddess recognized the Ox as a former acquaintance of the Heavenly realm and bowed to him. The Ox bowed his head in return and said, "We are both here at the pleasure of your father." In response to her puzzled look, the Ox explained the duplicity of the Jade Emperor, which had consigned the Ox to toil on earth, and caused his own youngest daughter to be wed to a mortal.

Since the young goddess wove beautiful cloth, "Seamstress" became her name. They lived in the straw hut built by the Cowboy and were very happy. Within three years, a baby boy and a baby girl joined the family.

One day, the Cowboy returned from working in the fields and found his children crying. Surprised that the Seamstress had not stopped their wailing, the Cowboy knelt and gathered them to his broad chest. "Now, now, stop crying and tell me why are you weeping, and where is your mother?"

Between tearful gasps, the boy told his father. "This...this morning, right...right after you...you left, a...a...a group of men came. They said...they said... they were messengers from the Jade Emperor and...and took mom with them. She did...did not want to go, but they...they grabbed her and...and took her anyway."

The Cowboy wiped their faces dry with his shirtsleeve, then carried the children to the Ox's shed. The Ox pondered the problem while chewing his cud. "It seems the Jade Emperor has finally found out about your taking his daughter for a wife and has sent his guards to get her back."

"But why did they wait so many years? Why did they not come seven years ago, when I first met her by the river?"

"That's because of the time difference. One day in the Heavenly realm is equivalent to one year in the mortal world. So even though she has lived with you for seven years, she was only missing for seven days in Heaven."

"How do I find her and get her back?"

"I don't know if you can get her back. But if you follow the Milky Way River to its headwaters in the mountains, it will lead you to the Heavenly Gate. Perhaps you can find some way to convince the Jade Emperor to let you into the Heaven and see her."

The stricken Cowboy looked at his crying children and straightened his back. "All right children, stop crying. We are going to look for your mother." The Cowboy placed the children in two woven bamboo baskets, and balancing the baskets on the ends of a long pole across his right shoulder, he started for the Milky Way River.

With thoughts of Seamstress, the Cowboy kept a fast pace. He felt stronger with every step toward the Milky Way. Finally, he climbed over the last mountaintop, but to his surprise, the great river was gone. Instead, a great endless desert had taken its place. Crestfallen, the Cowboy's last hope had disappeared without a trace. Lifting his tear-stained face, he noticed a bright shiny patch in the sky that had not been there before. After a second look, it dawned on him that it was the Milky Way. Sadly, he realized that the Jade Emperor had anticipated his move and pulled the Milky Way into the sky. Dejectedly, the Cowboy carried the children back to his straw hut.

He then told the Ox about the Milky Way's new place in the sky. The Ox sighed and lowered his great horned head in fatigue. "Young man, all these years you have been very kind to me and I have been very happy living with you. Now that I have spread my descendants in the mortal realm, I have accomplished my duty and soon I will pass from this realm. After I am gone, you can take my pelt and use it to make a cape. Now, don't object, I don't mind and I want you to do it. I was the one that told you about the

Seamstress. I used the two of you to get back at the Jade Emperor for tricking me into coming to live amongst the mortals.

"Now, it is only right that I atone for my sin of using you two as instruments of my vengeance by bringing you together again. Besides, it is the only way for you to see your wife again. When you put on the cape made from my skin, you will be able to fly into the sky and up into the Heaven." After saying those words, the Ox knelt to the ground, then rolled onto his side and stopped breathing.

The Cowboy used a sharp knife and carefully removed the pelt from the Ox's carcass. He then dug a grave in the garden. Solemnly, he buried the remains of the Ox's body, then burned fragrant incense and led the children in prayers over the grave. That night, under the shiny stars of the Milky Way, he sewed the oxhide into a large cape.

In the morning, the Cowboy put on the cape and picked up the two children. As he walked out of the door, he started drifting upward. Before long, the cape lifted him and the children like a kite in a draft of air. They soared over the fields, cities, rivers and mountains, then up into the clouds and beyond. Continuing higher, they flew past the moon and the sun, eventually reaching the shore of the Milky Way. As the Cowboy prepared to cross the great silvery river, its water started roiling, creating a towering wall of waves to block their advance. The Cowboy recognized it as another of the Jade Emperor's efforts to stop him from seeing the Seamstress.

By then, the Seamstress had heard about the Cowboy's visit into the Heaven. She drove a cloud chariot to the Heavenly court and begged to see the Jade Emperor. "Father, why will you not allow me to be with my husband and my children? They are your grandchildren."

"Because you are a goddess and he is a mortal. It is not a fitting match and I will not permit it," replied the Jade Emperor.

"But, did you not promise the Ox that if you lied to him, your daughter would be wed to a mortal?"

The Jade Emperor realized then that he had been outwitted by the "dumb" Ox. As a point of honor, he must keep his word and permit the Cowboy to reunite with the Seamstress. But, something had to be done to retain his dignity. As a compromise, he decreed that the Cowboy and the Seamstress should be allowed to reunite, but only for one day each year and only over the Milky Way, via a live flying bridge.

Ever since, on July seventh of each year, flocks of magpies join to form a bridge across the great Milky Way. The Cowboy and the Seamstress walk on the avian bridge to be united. On a clear night, up high in the sky near the great Milky Way, you can see two bright opposing stars, one of the stars has two smaller stars next to it. They are the Cowboy and the Seamstress, along with their two children. The Cowboy is the star with two smaller stars, for he has the two children with him.

Hence, the Chinese celebrate July seventh as the day for long parted lovers to be together again. On that particular day of the year, any raindrops that fall on earth are tears shed by the Cowboy and the Seamstress on the occasion of their reunion.

9
THE DRAGON MYTHOLOGY

		North/Winter 北·玄武 Black Tortoise	
	West/Summer 西·白虎 White Tiger	▲ ◄ 中　央 ► Center ▼	East/Spring 東·青龍 Green Dragon
		South/Fall 南·朱雀 Red Phoenix	

Chinese Geomancy Chart

There are four major divine creatures in Chinese mythology: the Dragon, who represents male yang energy; the Tiger, who represents vitality and prosperity; the Tortoise, who represents long life; and the Phoenix, which represents the female yin virtues.

In terms of geomancy—Feng Shui—the dragon favors aqua-green, the color of lively spring, and sits in the eastern direction. The tiger favors white, the color of hot summer, and sits in the western direction. The phoenix favors red, the color of falling leaves of fall and sits in the southern direction. Shuan Wu, the giant tortoise, who is often depicted with snake or dragon-like physical features, is the least prominent of the divine creatures. It favors black of dark winter and represents the northern direction. The dragon is the most popular of the four divine beings. Unlike the evilness that is usually associated with Western dragons, Chinese dragons are very gracious and desirable creatures. The Chinese consider dragons to be powerful supernatural demigods. They are rulers of the seas, lakes, and rivers and it is they that offer the rain to the earth and allow the crops to grow.

A typical Chinese dragon sports a beautiful pair of elongated stag horns atop his scaly head, two long tendrils arch from the end of a crocodilian snout. A thick serpentine body, and four giant chicken legs with sharp eagle talons at the toes complete the portrait. Although wingless, Chinese dragons can levitate through the air and swim in the deepest oceans. They are physically precise with exactly 117 scales; 81 of the scales are positive or *yang* and 36 scales are negative or *yin*. Their colors usually reflect their domains—rulers of oceans have deep blue scales, kings of lakes and ponds sport an aqua sheen on their bodies, and denizens of bogs and fens are muddy black.

Ordinary Chinese dragons have four toes—while the Imperial Dragon has five. During the Imperial Era, a golden, five-clawed dragon represents the Emperor. People refer to the imperial ruler as the "Dragon Personage." It is a capital offense for anyone other than the emperor to use the five-clawed dragon motif.

FABLES OF THE DRAGON: Tales of China

Chinese Imperial dragons have five toes on each foot. Indonesian dragons have four toes and Japanese dragons have three toes, because the further away from China a dragon travels the fewer toes it has. Dragons only exist in China, Korea, Indonesia, and Japan because if they traveled any further they would have no toes left to walk on. In modern times, the Chinese dragon has evolved to become the symbol of China.

The Chinese like to refer to a man of talent or heroism as a descendant of a dragon. It is not about genetic ties, but rather a euphemistic referral to a great ancestral heritage. The dragon is a benevolent representation of goodness, greatness, and blessings as well as all things divine and noble. People's high regard for dragons show in carvings, paintings, and writings, resulting in the dragons becoming the most popular and prevalent symbol of the land. In paintings, Chinese dragons are often depicted in misty clouds because normal humans cannot see a dragon in its entirety. Since they also warded off evil spirits and protected the innocent, Chinese dragons were known to represent good fortune and long life. They were often seen decorating the posts, beams, walls and rooftops of houses, temples, and palaces.

The Chinese believe that disasters—such as tidal waves, floods, and harsh storms are—the direct result of people upsetting the dragons.

The Sleeping Dragon in Shanghai
The construction of the city's Yan'an elevated highway (1995-1999) had been going relatively smoothly until reaching its hub point at the Chengdu Lu crossing. Oddly, defying all explanation, the digging crew's endless pounding couldn't budge the ground beneath the site for its central pillar. After a stream of engineers failed to figure out the cause of the delay, a priest was summoned to the site. At the end of the lengthy prayer and meditation, the priest informed the workers of a most unusual problem–a dragon

was sleeping beneath their work site. The construction had awakened it, and it was preventing the pillar from being installed. Dragons are proud creatures, the priest explained, so a simple yet noble gesture in its honor would restore its slumber allowing construction to continue. The workers complied, the pillar was erected and they all lived happily together.

Part II

The Book of Ladies

10

LǓ HÒU, THE FIRST EMPRESS

Lǚ Hòu (241—180 BC), was the first Empress of the Imperial Han Dynasty. She was also the first female ruler of China. Born as Lǚ Zhi, a commoner, she was an intelligent, loyal, obedient and considerate wife; but as an empress, she was ambitious, decisive, wise, and cruel to the point of being evil. As a visionary ruler, she created the foundation of a great empire. Her titled name, Lǚ Hòu, translate to Empress Lu.

When Lǚ married Liu Bang, he was a local ward officer. At the time, the laws of the Ch'in Empire were strict and unenforceable, but failure to enforce the law was a capital offense. Liu Bang chose to run off and join the bandits. During Liu Bang's absence, Lǚ farmed the land and sent food and supplies to her husband. Eventually, Lǚ was arrested and imprisoned for being the wife of an outlaw. In time, Lǚ was released from prison and joined her husband, who by then had risen to be a leader of the rebellion against the Ch'in.

During the struggle for power Lǚ along with her father-in-law, was taken captive and kept as a prisoner by Xiang Yu, another rebel leader. Xiang Yu was first an ally, but then became an opponent of Liu Bang. Xiang Yu threatened to boil Lǚ and her father-in-law if Liu Bang did not surrender. Liu Bang refused, and Xiang Yu being an honorable aristocrat did not carry out his threat. Lǚ was later released to rejoin her husband.

Years of campaigning, including two and half years as an enemy captive, traumatized Lǚ. They taught her the harsh realities of life and shaped her into a hard and bitter person who was paranoid about her safety. Then, to make it worse, she joined Liu only to learn that in her absence, he had taken a new concubine, Lady Qi. While Lǚ remained as the official wife, Lady Qi went with Liu whenever he went on campaigns.

After five years of fighting and hardship, Liu Bang persevered to become the First Emperor of the Han Dynasty, and Lǚ became the Empress. She remained fiercely loyal to her husband, but she took great lengths to protect her own position, and there were many threats to the new emperor and empress.

Liu had unified China, but his hold on the realms was tenuous, with much of the control in the hands of several powerful generals. The two most notable were Han Xin and Péng Yuè. At the Empress Lu's insistence and with her assistance, Liu Bang eliminated the two senior generals who had helped build the Han Empire. The empress made sure that not only the two generals were killed, but she also put to death their entire families to prevent future threats to the realm.

While Liu Bang was alive, Lǚ had schemed and struggled to protect her only son, Liu Ying and his position as the crown prince, because Liu Bang felt the crown prince was too timid. The emperor wanted to establish Prince Liu Ru Yi, a son by his favorite concubine Lady Qi, as the crown prince. The empress got four wise men to agree to serve as her son's tutor. She knew the emperor respected those four men and presented them as the crown prince's mentors. The maneuver vanquished any further effort to replace Liu Ying as the heir to the throne.

After the emperor died, Lǚ lost all restraint on her actions. She poisoned Prince Liu Ru Yi, then cut off Lady Qi's hands and feet, gouged out her eyes, smoked her ears to deafness, muted her with drugs, and then left her to die in the toilet. The empress made her son, the new emperor, watch the suffering of Lady Qi to toughen him for the rigors of being an emperor. The experience traumatized the seventeen-year-old boy. He refused to serve as the emperor, thus left Lǚ to rule the realm.

At the time, the death of Emperor Liu Bang left a power vacuum, and many powerful officials contemplated a coup to take over the empire. Lǚ knew of the budding threat, so she ordered all senior courtiers to observe Lady Qi's fate. The tortured woman endured for three days before she expired, and the coup attempt wilted. For the remainder of her reign, no one dared to challenge Empress Lǚ's authority.

The dowager empress wanted to bolster the position of her (Lǚ) family. She arranged the marriage of her eleven-year-old grandniece from the Lǚ family to the new emperor. When the young empress failed to produce an heir, Lǚ had the young girl pretend that she was pregnant and then claimed a newborn babe, Liu Gong, as her son. The new crown prince and imperial heir was actually fathered by the emperor and one of the concubines. Meanwhile, the real mother of the baby was put to death.

Seven years after ascending to the throne, Emperor Liu Ying died and the four-year-old Crown Prince Liu Gong became the emperor with Dowager Empress Lǚ as regent. In time, the young emperor learned of the circumstance of his true mother's death, and the impetuous youth swore to avenge his birth mother when he took power. Unfortunately for him, the dowager empress learned of his intentions and intervened. She murdered the ten-year-old emperor then set his brother Liu Hong as emperor, again with herself as regent.

Lǚ Zhi ruled the imperial palace with an iron fist but governed the realm with wise benevolence. She lowered taxes from twenty percent to seven percent, relaxed labor levies, and reformed the harsh penal code of the Ch'in dynasty. She strengthened the central government by eradicating the feudal hereditary fief practice; all officials were appointed by the central government. After over five hundred years of continuous warfare, the people finally had a respite to live in peace and prosperity.

In foreign policy, she favored diplomacy before force. Soon after Emperor Liu Bang's death, the nomadic Xiongnu chieftain Mao Dun sent an insulting letter to Empress Lǚ, "Your husband has just died, and my wife has also passed; we are two unhappy widowed rulers. I propose to offer my person to satisfy your needs." Empress Lǚ realized her realm was not ready for a war, she glossed over the insult and returned a diplomatic reply, "I am old and weak, with thinning hair and missing teeth, it would be most difficult for me to move about." Her return message was accompanied by rich gifts in horses and chariots. The elegant response avoided a bloody conflict and earned the respect of Mao Dun, who apologized for his discourtesy.

Empress Lǚ's attempt to install her family members in power created a power struggle between the Lǚ and the Liu clans, each with their own supporters in the imperial court. The attempt failed because the Lǚ clan members did not have sufficient time to consolidate their positions. In 180 BC, Empress Lǚ died of illness, and Liu loyalists massacred the Lǚ clan and their supporters and presented the throne to Liu Heng, a son of the first Han Emperor Liu Bang.

Empress Lǚ Zhi was a visionary ruler. Under her administration, the Han Empire prospered and grew strong, which laid the foundation for the first golden age of China, and one of the longest ruling dynasties (206 BC - 220 AD) of Chinese history. It was the reason that majority of the ethnic Chinese were called the Han people. Historians regard her as an effective ruler that made significant contributions to the building of China. Nevertheless, they referred to her as "The Manipulator."

11

WU ZE TIAN, THE FEMALE EMPEROR

Wu Ze Tian (624–705 AD), the first and only female emperor in Chinese history, was a beautiful, intelligent, ambitious, strong-willed, ruthless, and lusty woman. She fought through the gender-biased environment and rose to become one of the greatest emperors of China. Along the way to power she served two emperors, produced four sons and a daughter. Two of those sons became emperors before she took the throne for herself at the age of 65. As emperor she increased China's power, prestige, and borders; at the same time, she lived as a true imperial ruler with her stable of male concubines.

Wu entered the imperial palace at the age of fourteen as a concubine to Li Shi Min, the second emperor of the Imperial Tang Dynasty. She had the emperor's attention for a while but did not become one of his favorites. However, she devoted herself to literary studies in the palace and had the opportunity to serve as one of the emperor's attendants. The position allowed her to observe and learn the workings of the imperial court system and become acquainted with key officials of the palace. More importantly, she met and developed a personal relationship with the Crown Prince, Li Zhi.

In 649 AD, while Emperor Tai Zong (Li Shi Min) was on his deathbed, she was a personal attendant of the emperor. Wu was worried about her own fate. When the emperor died she would be sent to serve him in the afterlife, or to a nunnery. Only those concubines with royal children were allowed to continue living in the palace. To save herself, she seduced Crown Prince Li Zhi, who was four years her junior.

When the emperor died, Li Zhi ascended to the throne and took the name of Gao Zong. Wu, together with all other concubines without children, was sent to the imperial temple to live out her years as a nun. However, within a year, the new Emperor Gao Zong brought Wu Ze Tian back into the imperial palace as a concubine.

Soon, Wu realized she was a pawn in the game of court intrigue. The empress learned about the emperor's tryst with Lady Wu and encouraged him to bring Wu back into the palace. The empress was engaged in a fierce struggle against Lady Xiao for the emperor's favor. Wu would be used as a distraction to pry the emperor out of Lady Xiao's clutches.

The first phase of the empress' plan worked. The emperor began to spend more time away from Lady Xiao and kept company with the beautiful and caring Lady Wu. Emperor Gao Zong was weak-willed and indulged in the literary arts. Wu's literary talents in calligraphy and poetry endeared her to the young ruler. She would often encourage the emperor to spend more time attending to the affairs of the state instead of immersing himself in the literary arts. Her sense of priority and keen judgment gained the respect of the impressionable young emperor. Within no time, Wu Ze Tian became the emperor's favorite concubine and gave birth to a son, Li Hong.

Her rapid ascendency delighted the empress and infuriated Lady Xiao, however, the empress soon realized that she had brought a fox into the henhouse. She tried to change the balance of power with a shift in the alliance; she joined forces with Lady Xiao to counter Wu Ze Tian's influence on the emperor.

In 654 AD, while she was struggling for the emperor's favor, Lady Wu gave birth to a daughter. The empress paid a visit to the new princess. After her visit, the nursemaid found the baby dead. Wu blamed the empress for the murder of her daughter, but there was no proof except for the personal visit by the empress to the new princess. The incident alienated the empress from the emperor, but there was insufficient evidence to indict the accused. In the following year, the empress sought the help of sorcerers to win back the emperor's favor. The scheme backfired when Wu accused the empress of witchcraft, and in the ensuing investigation a doll in the image of the emperor was found under the empress' bed; it was an evidence of witchcraft, a serious offense. Based on Wu's accusation and the evidence, the emperor ousted the empress.

The emperor sought the advice of his ministers in choosing the next empress. Wu's prior acquaintances with courtiers came to her aid in the person of Senior Minister Li Khan. Li knew Emperor Tai Zong wanted Wu Ze Tian, and the minister suggested the emperor decide the issue on his own, as it is a person matter. When Wu became the empress, her aggressive dominance surged to the fore and she quickly intimidated the mild-mannered emperor, and there was no one to restrain her ambition.

Once secured in her position, Wu immediately took steps to eliminate potential oppositions; she imprisoned the ex-empress and Lady Xiao. Emperor Gao Zong despaired but chose not to oppose the empress' actions. When her spies told Wu that the emperor had secretly visited the two women, she had them sealed in a wall and starved them to death.

The emperor often suffered from migraine headaches, which left Wu as the de facto regent; and the empress used the time to consolidate her power. When the emperor went to Mount Tai to pay homage to the gods, she stepped to the fore and prayed to the gods together with the emperor; a not very proper act in the male-dominated regime.

In time, the emperor grew frustrated with her controlling dominance. In 664 AD, the emperor consulted with the prime minister to rein in the empress' growing power. However, Wu's spies informed her of the emperor's activities. She confronted the emperor with the allegation, and the weak-willed emperor blamed the whole episode on the prime minister. In the end, the prime minister and all male members of his family paid the penalty for the emperor's timidity.

Wu was cruel and vindictive to her enemies. Anyone she suspected to be a threat to her power was eliminated, to include her own sons. Wu Ze Tian had four sons. She poisoned the first when he opposed her maltreatment of Lady Xiao's daughters. She exiled the second son, and later had him commit suicide, when she suspected him of assassinating one of her confidants. She poisoned her own sister when the emperor took the woman into his bed. When the emperor bedded her niece (the deceased sister's daughter), she suffered the same fate as her mother.

In 683 AD, Emperor Gao Zong died and the third son Li Xian ascended to become Emperor Zhong Zong, but Wu Ze Tian retained power as the empress dowager and regent. Within a month, the emperor was removed for not being sufficiently obedient and compliant to the wishes of the dowager empress; thus, the youngest son became the new Emperor Rui Zong. In 690 AD, she browbeat the emperor into abdication then installed herself as the Emperor of the Imperial Tang Dynasty.

Emperor Wu was a willful but effective ruler, and China prospered under her reign. She championed the national examination system that searched for the most capable person for government positions. The system promoted individuals based on intelligence, merit, and scholarly knowledge, regardless of the person's heritage or background. She gave ample power to able and loyal subordinates.

She directed the installation of petition boxes for people to report on misdeeds of corrupt officials. She used the information submitted to investigate then oust old guard courtiers who opposed her position. The method removed many political opponents including the imperial uncle Chang-Sun Wu Ji, who was the prime minister. Chang-Sun was exiled then forced to commit suicide. The system effectively eliminated all threats to her power; however, the self-important arrogance of the prosecutors became a problem of its own. The emperor solved the problem with the expedient removal of the petition boxes, and the many prosecuting officials who did her dirty work. The excesses of the prosecuting officials had angered many people, thus their removal endeared the emperor to the people.

The emperor had a healthy appetite for men and maintained her own stable of male concubines. She did not, however, mix business with pleasure. One of her concubines refused to yield the right of way to the prime minister and was soundly beaten by the courtier's guardsmen for his arrogance and insubordination. The concubine cried to Wu Ze Tian and pleaded for vengeance. The emperor ascertained the situation then suggested that in the future the male concubine should avoid the routes used by the prime minister. When one of her concubines became overbearing or too much of an embarrassment, he would be dispatched minus a critical appendage placed atop his shoulder.

In 697 AD, at the age of seventy-three, Wu Ze Tian acquired a pair of handsome eighteen-year-old twin brothers into her stable; for their services to the realm, she made them kings with their own fiefs. They were the last of a long succession of her imperial bedmates.

In the spring of 705 AD, the eighty-one-year-old emperor fell seriously ill. A group of loyalists of the imperial Li family led by Li Xian–Wu Ze Tian's third son, that she had cast from the throne–launched a coup and restored the throne to the Li family. Wu Ze Tian was deposed, but she was allowed to retain her title without her political power. However, her twin concubines were not spared.

Emperor Wu was harsh but previous weak leadership was headed for factional power struggles between old guard courtiers, resulting in the inevitable decline of the empire. Wu Ze Tian's rise to power was opposed by an old guards faction led by the Prime Minister Chang-Sun Wu Ji. Emperor Wu removed the prime minister and his supporters then brought in a new crop of young and able courtiers who were responsible for resurrecting the empire. She laid the foundation for the second golden age of China, which lasted almost 300 years. Without Wu's intervention, the Imperial Tang Empire might have fallen quickly like its predecessor the Sui Dynasty, which lasted only thirty-seven years (581-618 AD).

Confucian scholars lambasted Wu for her incestuous relationship with her stepson, her ruthless persecution of her enemies and her amorous appetite. However, they could not deny her legacy as an effective and just ruler of the realm.

12

CI XI, THE LAST RULER OF IMPERIAL CHINA

In 1852, Ci Xi entered the imperial court of the Qing Dynasty as a concubine at the age of seventeen. She achieved prominence four years later when she gave birth to Crown Prince Zai Chun, the future Emperor Tong Zhi. Ci Xi was a skilled calligrapher. When Emperor Xian Feng fell ill he often relied on Ci Xi who read the daily reports to him and then wrote imperial edicts dictated by the emperor. At times the emperor even sought Ci Xi's opinion, to the distress of his ministers.

In 1860, Ci Xi followed the emperor out of Beijing as the combined Anglo-French force threatened the Capital. The emperor died in the following year, leaving the throne to the five-year-old Zai Chun, who assumed the name of Emperor Tong Zhi.

On his deathbed, Xian Feng left the realm in the hands of two groups—eight senior ministers who served as regent, and two queen-mothers who jointly controlled the imperial seal of office. He wanted the two groups to balance each other until Tong Zhi was old enough to assume the throne.

The eight ministers tried to control the realm, but Ci Xi had other ideas. She colluded with King Qin-Gong, the imperial uncle and younger brother of Emperor Xian Feng, in a coup d'état and arrested the eight ministers-regent. She killed the three most powerful ministers and fired the other five, thus made herself the dowager empress-regent. She rewarded Qin-Gong with an appointment as head of the powerful Military Affairs Office.

She employed ethnic Han Chinese in the imperial court to counter the Manchurian old guards of the court. The Han officials quelled the Taiping Rebellion and other ethnic revolts and stabilized the realm. She introduced western industries, initiated the modernization of the military to strength and revive the empire. In 1873, Emperor Tong Zhi turned 18 and Ci Xi turned the reign of power over to the young emperor; however, the dowager empress could not help but interfere in the affairs of the state. When the emperor fired all of his senior officials for opposing his wishes, Ci Xi intervened to force a retraction of the edict.

Emperor Tong Zhi died of illness in 1875, and Ci Xi returned to power as the Dowager Empress/Regent. She chose her four years old nephew Zai Tian as the new emperor—who took the name of Emperor Guang Xu.

King Qin-Gong, the minister of military affairs, became the leader of the pro-westernization faction of the court, which was opposed by the old guard traditionalist faction. Ci Xi played the two factions against each other. In 1884, Ci Xi fired all senior officials at the Military Affairs Office, which included King Qin-Gong and other leaders of the pro-west faction and blamed them for the French success against the Qing army in Vietnam. The maneuver eliminated the greatest political threat to Ci Xi's position. Five years later, Emperor Guang Xu got married and formally assumed the role of the emperor. Ci Xi officially turned over the rein of power, but in reality maintained a firm grip on the workings of the imperial court.

In 1894 Japan invaded the Chinese protectorate of Korea which led to the Sino-Japanese War. China declared war to defend its protectorate against the Japanese invasion. Initially, Ci Xi favored war with Japan, however, it coincided with the coming celebration of her 60th birthday. She appropriated the navy's operational funds to renovate the Imperial Garden—Yuan He Yuan. When Japan defeated China on land and at sea, Ci Xi supported the dove faction to sign a peace treaty with Japan, so as to minimize the war's impact on her birthday celebrations. Ci Xi ceded Liao-Dong Peninsula, Taiwan, Korea, Pescadores, and opened up four more ports for foreign commerce, and paid two billion ounces of silver to Japan as war indemnities.

The Sino-Japanese war launched the foreign colonization of China, which engendered the political reformation movement by Chinese progressive elements. Ci Xi initially supported the movement to strengthen China, but she kept a tight rein on the military and political powers. In June 1898, Emperor Guang Xu issued the National Strategic Edict to reform the empire. The strategy infringed on the interests of the old guard Manchu aristocrats and Mandarin courtiers. They joined forces and opposed the progressive reform measures. Ci Xi allied with the old guards and launched a coup d'état. She placed Emperor Guang Xu under house arrest and executed six ringleaders of the reformation movement.

Ci Xi had no sooner regained power before the Boxer Rebellion raised its ugly head. Efforts to put down the rebellion failed, and the Boxers spread into Beijing. Ci Xi attempted to quell and pacify the Boxers at the same time, while the eight foreign powers (Austro-Hungary, Britain, France, Germany, Italy, Japan, Russia and the United States) insisted on bringing their troops into Beijing. Ci Xi decided to use the Boxers to counter the foreign powers. She encouraged the Boxers to assault foreign embassies, at the same time she dispatched emissaries to each embassy requesting their assistance and intervention to resolve the crisis. In August of 1900, armies of the eight foreign powers entered Beijing, and Ci Xi fled with Emperor Guang Xu to Xi-An. She ordered a negotiated peace with the invaders and blamed the Boxers for the invasion. The foreign invasion cost China 9.8 billion ounces of silver in war indemnities, countless deaths and suffering of the people, demolition of all artillery positions from the coast to Beijing, and removal of pro-war officials.

On October 6th, 1901 she started her return trip to Beijing with three thoussand baggage carts and an entourage of 10's of 1000's of guards and other courtiers. The procession arrived at Beijing on January 8th of the following year. To placate the rebellious public, she ordered the institution of "New Administration" for economic, military, education, government, and other reforms. An Imperial Outline of Constitution, modeled after the German and Japanese constitutions, was published in 1908 to retain the imperial reign.

On October 14th, 1908, Emperor Guang Xu died, and Ci Xi followed him to the nether realm a day later.

Ci Xi was intelligent, willful, devious, and power hungry. She manipulated various factions to preserve her power in a male-dominated environment. Many Chinese held her responsible for the Century of Humiliation (1839-1949) suffered by China, as she was the person in charge for a great portion of that era. Her ever-changing decisions certainly added fuel to the opinion of a shallow minded, scheming woman who placed her personal interests above that of the people and the realm. The use of naval funds during wartime to build her imperial garden for her birthday bash and the Boxer Rebellion fiasco were her most notable faux pas.

Ci Xi did contribute to the women's cause in China. She forbade foot binding and promoted schools for educating women.

She was the last of the three female rulers of China. Her legacy was the Century of Humiliation, which started with the Opium War and ended with the communist takeover of China. She was also the one that chose the peony as the national flower of China. She was a diametric contrast to the two strong women who had ruled China earlier—Lu Hou of the Han Dynasty and Wu Ze Tian of the Tang Dynasty. The two earlier female rulers expanded and made China great, while Ci Xi abetted in the downfall of the Chinese empire.

13
MO XI, THE TEMPTRESS

King Si Lu-Gui (Circa 1652 -1600 BC) was the seventeenth and last ruler of the Xia Dynasty. Known as Jie The Cruel, he was a strict and tyrannical ruler. When the Yo Shi tribe failed to send tribute to the Xia kingdom. Under the threat of a massacre, the tribal chief presented his sister Mo Xi to King Jie as a peace offering. The king accepted the gift and recalled his army.

Mo Xi mesmerized the king, who did everything he could to please his new concubine. She liked to hear the sound of ripping silk; so the king had yards of fine silk brought in daily only to be torn up in her presence to produce the entertaining sound.

King Jie made her his queen and built a new palace in the style of her homeland for the new queen. At her request, the king drafted three thousand pretty women to dance and entertain at the palace. So, in addition to the silk used for her daily pleasure, the people also had to produce three thousand silk robes for the dancing girls.

The king liked to demonstrate his superiority as a great warrior; at his royal banquets, he often had people kneel so that he could sit on their backs and entertain his wife and guests.

However, with the passing of time, King Jie found new love interests. They came in the form of two beautiful women that the king's army brought back from the recently conquered Min Shan tribe. The king became enamored with his newly acquired trophies. His endless revelry and pleasure-seeking came at the expense of neglecting affairs of the state and the queen.

Around 1600 BC, Lord Tang of the Shang state led a rebellion which overthrew the Xia dynasty and he became the first ruler of the Shang dynasty. It was only afterward that people realized Mo Xi's odd behaviors such as tearing of silk, lavish constructions, and grand feasts were part of her brother's grand scheme to destroy the Xia kingdom. They were all designed to empty the Xia treasury and enrage the people against the realm.

Woven fine silk was labor intensive and expensive, their wanton destruction outraged the feudal lords and the populace. Construction of the new palace further taxed the treasury and inflamed the anti-government sentiment of the people. Finally, she collaborated with the First Minister of the Shang state to pass on information to the rebellious Lord Tang.

Unfortunately for Mo Xi, Lord Tang did not appreciate her contribution in overthrowing Jie. Her reputation as a wanton woman with odd habits and a history of disloyalty to her king was not desired in the new Shang realm. The new king banished Jie to live at the shore of the eastern ocean with Mo Xi to keep him company.

Mo Xi was the first of many women in Chinese history who used their beauty and wiles to bedazzle a ruler and topple his realm. Chinese scholars coined the phrase, "Painted Faces are Troubled Waters," to describe Mo Xi and other women of her ilk. She was also the first female spy of Chinese history. She ranked as the first of the Four Evil Women of Chinese Folklore because historians blamed her for toppling the Xia Dynasty; the first royal dynasty of ancient China.

14
DA JI, THE CRUEL QUEEN

In 1047 BC, King Xin of the Shang Dynasty invaded the Yo Su people. Among the war trophies was Su Da Ji, daughter of the Yo Su tribal chieftain. The elderly king doted on the young concubine and made her queen of the kingdom. He valued everything she liked and abhorred anything that displeased her. He even banished his own son, Crown Prince Yin Jiao, to please the young queen.

The king built a special palace, Lǔ Tai, to entertain her. It had a wine filled pond that could swim horses and groves of hanging meat. Feasts at the palace often had three thousand participants. Guests would drink from the pond and eat off the meat groves. The king often ordered his guests to disrobe and participate in orgies to liven the revelry.

Da Ji was cruel and vengeful. One of the king's concubines was the daughter of Lord Jiu, a grand duke of the realm. The woman disapproved of the debauchery and the orgies and spoke against such behavior. The outspoken concubine paid for her brashness with her life and that of her father. Lord Jiu was boiled into the stew and distributed to the other lords. Lord E (pronounced as Er), another grand duke, denounced the treatment of Lord Jiu and was turned into jerked meat for his troubles. The third grand duke Chang, Lord of the Western Provinces, sighed privately at the depravity of the king. Unfortunately, the sigh was overheard and reported to the king, and Chang became a guest in the king's prison.

King Xin's barbaric behavior caused resentment, resulting in vicious punishments for the malcontents and the queen devised cruel ways to torture the prisoners. She ordered prisoners chained to large bronze posts then set a fire at its base and roasted the prisoners to death. Other prisoners were made to walk on the oiled bronze post over a bed of hot coal. Prisoners inevitably fell off the post and into the fire. Their screams brought peals of laughter from Da Ji.

In 1046 BC, King Xin launched another expedition against his southeastern neighbors. Lord Ji Fa, son of Chang, took the opportunity to summon his allies and attacked the Shang Capital at Cao-Ge with three hundred chariots, royal guards, and men-at-arms. With his army away in the southeast, the king armed slaves and former prisoners-of-war and led them to defend the realm from Lord Ji Fa. The two armies met at Mu-Ye forty lis (seven miles) outside of the capital. Although outnumbered by more than three-to-one, the rebel army smashed the loyalist force; at the onset of the battle, a large number of the slaves and former prisoners turned against the king and joined the rebel army.

King Xin fled to Lǚ Tai, where he set the building afire. When the rebel army arrived, he donned his finest robes and jewelry and then threw himself into the flames. Da Ji was caught and executed; although some historians said she was taken as a concubine by Duke Zhou, a brother of Lord Ji Fa. The death of King Xin marked the end of the Shang dynasty and the beginning of the Zhou dynasty.

Da Ji was blamed for the downfall of the Shang dynasty, which earned her the infamous title as the Second Most Evil Woman of Chinese Folklore.

15
BAO SI, THE SMILE THAT TOPPLED A KINGDOM

Bao Si was another early temptress of Chinese history. In 779 BC, the thirteen-year-old Bao Si was already famous for her beauty. The Lord of the Bao state sent her to King You of the Zhou kingdom as a gift.

The king adored the beautiful concubine and doted on her. Although pretty, her temperament would frost over the warmest heart; she rarely if ever smiled. The king tried every means possible to get her to laugh, without success. It became an obsession for him to get the concubine to smile. To please the pretty woman, the king removed Queen Shen and installed Bao Si as the new queen. He removed Crown Prince Yi Jiu and named Bao Si's son Bo Fu as the new crown prince. But, Bao Si remained cold and unsmiling.

Finally, King You offered a thousand pieces of gold to anyone that could make Bao Si smile. Minister Hu Shi-Fu suggested that the king light the smoke signal at Li-Shan in the western border region. The king thought about it and ordered the fire at the watchtower lit as recommended. At the sight of the smoke signal, all the feudal lords of the land answered the summons; they gathered their armies and marched to Li-Shan to fight the invaders. On arrival, the lords found the king sitting atop the fortress, having a feast with Bao Si.

They realized there was no threat to the kingdom; the king had only summoned them to entertain the queen. The lords marched home in anger; however, the hasty arrival and rueful departure of the grand armies did make Bao Si break into laughter.

The deposed Queen Shen fled home with her son Yi Jiu to her father at the Shen state. In 771 BC, Lord Shen summoned the lords of Zeng and Lǚ states then invited the nomadic Quan Rong tribe to join them in invading Gao-Jing, the Capital of the Zhou kingdom. King You lit the smoke signal to summon help, but the lords thought it was yet another trick by the king and no one went to the rescue.

The Quan Rong army sacked Gao-Jing, killed King You and Crown Prince Bo Fu then took Bao Si prisoner. The loyalist lords finally arrived with their armies to Gao-Jing and drove away Quan Rong and the rebel lords; Bao Si was left behind to fend for herself. Fearing retribution from the collective loyalist lords, Bao Si hung herself. So ended the life of the Third Most Evil Woman of Chinese Folklore.

In 770 BC, the victorious lords installed Prince Yi Jiu as the new king of the Zhou dynasty, who took the name of King Ping. King Ping decided Gao-Jing was beyond repair and moved the Capital east to Wang-Cheng. Duke Xiang of Ch'in had been the major force in ejecting the Quan Rong nomads from Gao-Jing. He escorted the new king to Wang-Cheng. In appreciation, King Ping gave Duke Xiang the western territories that became the Ch'in state.

The move of the Capital to Wang-Cheng marked the beginning of the East Zhou Dynasty. In historical context, it was also the beginning of the Spring and Autumn Era, when the power of the Zhou kingdom started its decline and feudal lords began power struggles that fragmented the realm into scores of kingdoms. Five hundred and forty-nine years later, in 221 BC, after centuries of continuous warfare, King Zheng—a scion of Duke Xiang—reunified the land and created the Imperial Ch'in Empire.

In retrospect, Bao Si indirectly enabled the creation of China. For, without Bao Si, the Quan Rong nomads would not have been able to sack Gao-Jing, and Duke Xiang would never have acquired the Ch'in state; the state which eventually vanquished the other kingdoms and united China. Even the name China originated from the Imperial Ch'in Empire.

The ancient watchtower that King You lit the smoke signal to amuse Bao Si still stands at Li-Shan in Shaanxi province.

Chinese scholars used Bao Si's story to coin the term "A smile that toppled a kingdom," to describe the looks of a beautiful woman.

16

LI JI, THE SCHEMER

In 663 BC, Duke Xian of the Ghin kingdom conquered the Li Rong state and took two daughters of the king as war booties. The elder princess, Li Ji gave birth to a son named Xi Qi, and the younger princess had a boy named Zho Zi.

Duke Xian adored Li Ji and when the Duke's wife died, Li Ji became his wife, while her sister was made a senior concubine.

The ambitious new duchess wanted her son to inherit the dukedom, but the duke already had a crown prince, Shen Sheng. She bribed two ministers of the court, Liang Wu and Bi Wu, and had them persuade the duke to dispatch the crown prince and his two brothers, Chong Er and Yi Wu, to outlying posts of Qu-Wuo, Pu-Cheng and Nan-Bei-Qu respectively.

With the three princes out of the way, Li Ji started working on Duke Xian. She pointed out that the crown prince was working on gathering supporters and might plot a coup to overthrow the duke. The duke felt that the crown prince was working on winning the hearts and minds of the people, but he would never contemplate anything against his own father.

Undaunted, Li Ji persuaded the duke to summon the crown prince. Shen Sheng returned to meet his father then visited Li Ji to pay his respects. She had the crown prince remain for dinner with her. That night, she cried and complained to the duke that the crown prince teased her during his visit. She said the crown prince even joked about the duke being too old for her, but the duke did not believe her. Li Ji said she would prove it on the next day.

In the morning, the Duchess sent for the crown prince to accompany her to the zoo. Beforehand, she smeared honey in her hair. When bees hovered over the honey infused hair, she requested Shen Sheng's help in fending off the bees. The crown prince used his long sleeve to shoo off the bees, which were observed by the duke from a tower not far away from them.

Her act convinced the duke of the crown prince's guilt. The angry duke was about to arrest and execute the crown prince, but Li Ji pleaded for Shen Sheng's life. She said, "I was the one that invited the crown prince, should he die the blood would be on my hands. Nobody else knows about this, I think we should let it pass." The duke relented but evicted the crown prince out of the palace.

One day, the crown prince sent a piece of sacrificial meat to the duke. Li Ji had a man lace poison on the meat then blamed Shen Sheng for trying to murder his father. Saddled with overwhelming evidence, the crown prince hung himself to atone for the misdeed. Li Ji then convinced the duke that Chong Er and Yi Wu were in on the plot with Shen Sheng. It forced the two princes to flee out of the country.

With the three princes gone, Li Ji got Duke Xian to name her son Xi Qi as the Crown Prince. In 652 BC, the duke died and Xi Qi inherited the throne. However, the Ghin senior ministers did not approve of Li Ji's manipulations of the power structure. Minister Li Keh led a coup and executed the young duke then invited Prince Yi Wu to return and inherit the dukedom.

Two years later, Da Ji's role in the murder of Crown Prince Shen Sheng was uncovered, and she too was executed.

Da Ji ranked last among the Four Evil Women of Chinese Folklore.

17
XI SHI, THE SUNKEN FISH

In 494 BC, King Fu Chai of the Wu kingdom, in eastern central China, conquered the Yue kingdom. The vanquished king and his wife became slaves in Fu Chai's stable, responsible for the care of animals and the royal horse carriage. However, King Gou Jian was allowed to retain an entourage of loyal courtiers from his old royal court. Among them were Wen Tsong and Fan Li, who had been ministers of the Yue court and were leaders of Gou Jian's loyalists.

The Yue courtiers mapped a strategy to revive the Yue kingdom. The first step was to earn Fu Chai's trust so that he would release Gou Jian to his homeland. One day, when Fu Chai fell ill, Gou Jian willingly tasted the feces of the king, to help determine the ailment, and thus demonstrated his loyalty to Fu Chai. Three years after their entry into bondage, Wen Tsong bribed Bo Pee, the Wu Prime Minister, who persuaded King Fu Chai to order the release of Gou Jian, over the dissent of General Wu Tze Shu of the Wu kingdom.

Upon returning home, Gou Jian set about avenging the defeat. The king slept on brushwood and licked a gallbladder that hung from a beam before each meal to remind him of the bitterness and humiliations his country suffered. At Wen Tsong's suggestion, Gou Jian commissioned men to search far and wide for beautiful women.

Xi Shi, whose beauty was renowned throughout the land, was chosen along with another beauty named Zheng Dan. Fan Li trained the women in court etiquette, singing, dancing and playing musical instruments. He then personally escorted the ladies to Gu Su, the Capital of the Wu kingdom as tribute gifts from Gou Jian. During the journey, Xi Shi and Fan Li fell in love with each other; they pledged mutual eternal love, to be consummated at a future date.

King Fu Tsai became infatuated with the female courtesans sent by Gou Jian, and they persuaded the king to relax his vigilance against the Yue people.

In 486 BC, Fu Chai attacked the Qi kingdom to expand his realm. Gou Jian used the opportunity to demonstrate his loyalty to the Wu state, and he sent an army to aid Fu Tsai's force. The ensuing victory further reinforced Fu Tsai's trust of Gou Jian. Four years later, in 482 BC, Fu Chai led his army to join an alliance of armies against the neighboring Jin kingdom in the northeast and left his homeland in the charge of his son, Crown Prince Yu.

Xi Shi sent word to inform Gou Jian that Gu Su was garrisoned by old men and feeble troops. Thus, while Fu Chai and his army were victorious in battle against the Jin, his kingdom came under attack from Gou Jian. The Wu garrison force was too weak and unprepared against the vengeful Yue army. Crown Prince Yu died in battle and his army was decimated. Fu Chai rushed home to confront the Yue invaders, but was unable to defeat Gou Jian; however, the Yue King realized he was not yet strong enough to conquer the Wu kingdom, thus agreed to an armistice then withdrew his troops.

Ten years later, in 473 BC, Gou Jian returned with a stronger army and soundly defeated Fu Chai's force. This time, it was the Wu King who sued for peace and Gou Jian wavered, but Fan Li, the commanding general, objected; he reminded Gou Jian of the folly of Fu Chai's foolish leniency twenty years ago. "When you wish to eradicate the weed, you must pull it out by the roots." Finally, the Wu King rued the day that he did not kill Gou Jian and committed suicide.

Xi Shi returned home into the arms of Fan Li, who resigned his senior court position and retired to enjoy his life with the beautiful woman that he had loved but could not hold for seventeen long years. The famous Xi Hu (West Lake) in Hang-Zhou was said to have been named after Xi Shi. She was also the subject of numerous poems by famous Chinese poets such as Li Bai and Su Dong Po.

Xi Shi was graced with the nickname of "Sunken Fish" because she had originally been a wash woman. Allegedly, when she was working by the creek, her beauty so bedazzled the fish that they forgot to swim and sank to the bottom of the water. However, there was one flaw in Xi Shi's good looks. She had oversized feet and was ashamed of that blemish. Xi Shi liked to dance to show off her fine form and artistic talent but was loathe at the need to display her feet. To hide her oversized appendages, Xi Shi had specially designed platform shoes made, so that when she danced, people would only see the ends of her footwear. They were the world's first pair of high heels or platform shoes.

Xi Shi was renowned in Chinese folklore as the first of Four Great Beauties of Chinese Folklore. Because Xi Shi had initially been a wash-woman, she was, therefore, most frequently depicted washing cloth by the river bank.

18

WANG ZHAO JUN, THE FALLEN GEESE

Wang Zhao Jun was born in 52 BC, during the Han Dynasty (206 BC - 220AD). Hers was one of the best-known tales of "political marriages" in Chinese history. She was the also the first documented case of the tradition that Chinese emperors bought border peace with Chinese princesses.

Wang Zhao Jun came from an aristocratic family. She was chosen, at the age of 16, for her renowned beauty to enter the imperial harem during the reign of Emperor Yuan of the Western Han Dynasty (48-33 BC).

Chinese emperors traditionally maintained a harem of three thousand courtesans; to simplify the selection process of the nightly companion, the emperor would review catalogs of the (courtesan's) portraits. Therefore, it became customary for palace ladies to bribe court artists so that they painted the most enticing portraits. Wang Zhao Jun, however, was confident of her natural beauty and refused to pay the court painter, Mao Yan-Shou, the customary bribe. As a result, her finished portrait did not attract the emperor's attention, and she never received the imperial favor.

Wang Zhao Jun languished in the imperial palace for three years and expected to die an old maid. Because once a maiden entered the palace, she became a member of the emperor's household and could not leave without the ruler's permission. However, an opportunity came in the form of the nomadic Xiongnu, ancestors of Attila the Hun. In 33 BC, Huan Xie, the Xiongnu chieftain agreed to become a subject of the Imperial Han Empire; he requested a Han princess to be his wife. Emperor Yuan consented and solicited a volunteer among his courtesans.

Wang Zhao Jun volunteered to marry Huan Xie. When the lady-in-charge of the harem sent the unflattering portrait of Wang Zhao Jun to the palace, the emperor glanced at the unflattering portrait then nodded his approval of the candidate for the marriage.

At the presentation ceremony, Emperor Yuan saw the true beauty of Wang Zhao Jun, but it was too late to change his mind. Ruefully, the emperor decreed Wang Zhao Jun as an Imperial Princess and personally sent her off with twenty-eight thousand bolts of silk, sixteen thousand pounds of cotton, plus a large amount of gold, jade and other valuable jewelry as dowry to the Xiongnu. Huan Xie and his people were overjoyed with their beautiful new queen and the bountiful gift. The marriage of Wang Zhao Jun to Huan Xie was instrumental in maintaining the peace between the two realms. For the next sixty years, no smoke signals were lit from watchtowers atop the Great Wall.

Emperor Yuan was incensed at losing Wang Zhao Jun, and Mao Yan-Shou paid for his greed with his life. Thereafter, Mao Yan Shou's name became a term that was synonymous with a corrupt and greedy government official.

Wang Zhao Jun acquired the nickname of the "Fallen Geese" because when she was traveling across the Gobi Desert to her new home, a wild goose that flew by saw the beautiful maiden, forgot about flying thus fell to the ground. Fallen Geese's blemish in her beauty was her supposedly too narrow shoulders. Wang Zhao Jun often wore a padded robe or heavy coat to hide the blemish in her looks. Her padded robe was probably another historical first. She was also an excellent musician with the pipa, a four-stringed lute-like instrument. Paintings of Wang Zhao Jun usually depict her wearing a heavy fur coat to broaden her shoulders while carrying a pipa in her arms.

Wang Zhao Jun was renowned in Chinese folklore as the second of Four Great Beauties of Chinese Folklore.

19
DIAO CHAN, THE HIDDEN MOON

Diao Chan lived around 190 AD, during the latter part of Eastern Han Dynasty (25-220 AD). She was a beautiful courtesan of Wang Yun, a junior minister of the Imperial Han court. He had despaired at the way that Dong Zhuo, the Prime Minister, dominated the imperial court. It would be only a matter of time before the prime minister overthrew the emperor and took the dragon seat for himself. One day, after witnessing another blatant murder of a courier by Dong Zhuo, the junior minister contrived on a scheme to be rid of the prime minister.

Wang Yun joined Dong Zhuo's political faction then secretly promised to give the beautiful Diao Chan to Lǚ Bu, the most valiant warrior of the realm; who was also the ward and trusted henchman of Dong Zhuo. Then, on the pretext of seeking Dong Zhuo's favor, Wang Yun presented Diao Chan to the Prime Minister as a gift.

Lǔ Bu was infatuated with the courtesan and could not force himself to give her up. One day, while Dong Zhuo was at court, Lǔ Bu entered Diao Chan's quarters and invited her into the garden, where the courtesan professed her love for the young warrior and bemoaned the ill treatment she received from the short and obese prime minister. Dong Zhuo returned home to find Diao Chan in Lǔ Bu's arms. The prime minister snatched up Lǔ Bu's halberd and stabbed at the young man. Lǔ Bu easily evaded the thrust and escaped from the residence. Lǔ Bu and Dong Zhuo eventually reconciled, but a schism had been created between them.

Wang Yun took advantage of the rift and recruited Lǔ Bu into the anti-Dong Zhuo clique. Wang Yun disguised a dozen men in the uniform of the imperial guard. The men ambushed the prime minister as he was on his way to the imperial court. Dong Zhuo called on Lǔ Bu for aid, but Lǔ Bu pulled out an imperial edict that sentenced the prime minister to death. Lǔ Bu's act froze the men that had been protecting Dong Zhuo, and the prime minister was hacked to death.

In the aftermath of Dong Zhuo's death, Wang Yun assumed power and became arrogant. He ruthlessly eliminated Dong Zhuo's supporters. His arrogance and brutality caused estrangement from his political allies. The factional schism provided an opening for Dong Zhuo loyalists who plotted a counter-strike and successfully captured then killed Wang Yun. Those same people blamed Diao Chan for complicity in Dong Zhuo's downfall and put her to death.

Diao Chan was known as "Hidden Moon" because when she prayed at night, her beauty put the Moon to shame so that it had to take refuge in the clouds. Diao Chan was often depicted praying under the cloud darkened moon wearing gaudy earrings; the earrings were meant to disguise and distract people from noticing her natural defect of small earlobes.

Diao Chan ranked third among the Four Great Beauties of Chinese Folklore.

20

YANG YU HUAN, THE WILTED FLOWER

Yang Yu Huan (719-756 AD), better known as Yang Gui Fei—Precious Lady Yang—lived during the Tang Dynasty (618-907 AD). She was the youngest and the most famous of the Four Great Beauties of Chinese Folklore. She was originally the wife of Li Mao, the eighteenth son of Emperor Xuan Zong. The emperor had just lost his favorite courtesan to illness. He wanted Yang Yu Huan for himself. He first ordered her to become a priestess to serve in the temple honoring the emperor's mother; the estranged husband (Li Mao) was directed to remarry. Afterward, Xuan Zong recalled Yang Yu Huan into the palace to be his concubine. He appointed her as Yang Gui Fei or Precious Lady Yang. At the time, he was sixty-one and she was twenty-seven. Her elevated position enabled various members of her family to become senior imperial courtiers.

Her cousin, Yang Guo Zong, became the Prime Minister; her uncle Yang Xuan Gui received a senior position in the capital; her brother, Yang Xian was appointed as a minister of the second rank; and her three sisters were all named as Ladies of the Imperial Court.

Prior to her arrival on the scene, China had enjoyed thirty years of peace and prosperity under the benevolent rule of Emperor Xuan Zong. The old emperor doted on his new love and neglected his obligations to the realm. He was an accomplished composer and spent long hours being entertained by Yang Yu Huan. The emperor left the nation in the hands of Yang Gui Fei's uncle, cousin, and brothers, who led a clique of corrupt officials that brought ruin and destruction to the empire.

In 755 AD, An Lǔ Shan, an imperial general of nomadic descent, rebelled and marched into the imperial capital of Chang-An. Emperor Xuan Zong fled southwest with his entourage.

They had not gone far from the capital when the soldiers halted at Ma-Wei Hill and refused to go on. They blamed the Yang family for the chaotic state of the empire and executed Yang Guo Zong, the prime minister. The troops then demanded the death of Yang Gui Fei. Reluctantly, Emperor Xuan Zong ordered two eunuchs to strangle Yang Gui Fei with a length of white silk sash. At the time, she was only thirty-eight years old.

Some people said a servant girl was substituted for Yang Gui Fei at Ma-Wei Hill. Supposedly, Precious Lady Yang survived and fled to Japan. In the Yamaguchi prefecture of Japan, there is a tomb of Yang Yu Huan. In 1963, a Japanese lady claimed to be a descendant of Precious Lady Yang, the Japanese woman presented a family tree ledger which listed Yang Gui Fei as her ancestor.

Yang Gui Fei was known as "Wilted Flower" because once, when she entered the imperial garden, she touched a flower which immediately wilted at the attention from the beautiful courtesan. Precious Lady Yang supposedly had stronger body odor, which was the reason she took frequent sulfur spring baths, as an attempt to cover up her feminine aroma. Her frequent bathing is the reason that she was the only famous woman of Chinese antiquity to be depicted in the nude in paintings and statues.

A traditional Chinese beauty was usually described as oval faced with square shoulders and a willow like body. Yang tended toward the Rubenesque side, and her name is often used when referring to a full-bodied female.

Yang Yu Huan is renowned as the last of the Four Great Beauties of Chinese Folklore.

21

PRINCESS WEN CHENG, THE QUEEN OF TIBET

In 634 AD, King Songtsän Gampo united Tibet and sent an envoy to the court of the Imperial Tang Empire. The king wanted a Tang princess for his bride. Emperor Tai Zong refused, and the irate king of Tibet responded by attacking Qinghai. The king's army was defeated, but he managed to extract a princess out of the ensuing peace treaty.

In 641 AD, Princess Wen Cheng, a distant relative of the emperor, arrived in Tibet for her marriage to the king. Wen Cheng brought with her promises of trade agreements and safe passage on the Silk Road, and a dowry worthy of an imperial princess. It included gold, fine furniture, silks, porcelains, books, jewelry, musical instruments, three hundred and sixty rolls of Buddhist scriptures and medical books. In addition, her large entourage of artisans and craftsmen introduced new crops, farming methods, tools, agricultural technology, metallurgy, weaving looms, construction techniques, manufacture of paper and ink, as well as developing the Tibetan alphabet and writing system.

Her marriage brought forty years of peace and tranquility between the two people. She was responsible for introducing Buddhism into Tibet. The Jokhang temple in Lhasa still houses the statues of Buddha which she carried into Tibet.

Wen Cheng's legacy and influence live on in Tibet. On the fifteenth day of the fourth month and the fifteenth day of the tenth month of each Tibetan year, Tibetans sing and dance in her honor. Historic relics such as statues of King Songtsän Gampo with Princess Wen Cheng still stand on display for worship by all in the Potala Palace in Lhasa. Their sleep chamber remains preserved in the palace. Frescos inside the palace are filled with scenes depicting her travels to Tibet and the marriage to the Tibetan king. The original Tang willow trees in front of the Jokhang temple were planted by Princess Wen Cheng. In the Tibetan Buddhist religion, she is revered as the Guan Yin goddess reincarnate.

22

ZHONG-LI CHUN, THE UGLY QUEEN

Around 312 BC, a woman walked up to the royal palace of Lin-Tse and requested an audience with the king. The guards asked her about the purpose of the audience, and she replied, "I am an ugly spinster of this country, and I would offer myself to be the king's consort." The guards were surprised by her pronouncement, not only because of her looks, but also because the king had only recently beheaded his queen.

King Shuan of the Qi kingdom was having a banquet. He was amused by the demand of the bold woman and decided to let her be the entertainment for his guests. The court erupted in gasps and laughter as the middle-aged woman presented herself to the king. The only normal part about the woman was her height. She had a protruding forehead, sunken sleepy eyes, upturned rain-catcher nostrils, a fat head with thinning hair, thick neck knotted by a man-sized Adam's apple, and a stout body supported by hefty limbs, all covered with a layer of mottled dark-reddish skin.

The king waited until the court to fell silent then gestured for her to sit before asking, "You said you wanted to be my wife? My palace teems with beauties, while your owns villagers would shun you. What special talents have you, that I should accept your suit?"

The woman took her time and sat cross-legged on her cushion, she placed her hands on her knees then bowed to the king, "Great king, I am Zhong-Li Chun of Wu-Yan county. I am thirty, and yet unwed. The country is in great danger and I am here to rescue it."

"Go on, and explain," said the perplexed king.

"First, the powerful Ch'in kingdom threatens from the west, while we face the Chu foe in the south; you have corrupt officials holding sway in your court, causing discontentment among the people; and you did not name a crown prince, leaving the future of the state in limbo. Second, you built towering palaces that caused hardship and a heavy tax on the people. Third, you have driven away honorable men, while fawning officials roam free. Lastly, you indulge in continuous womanizing and debauchery, at the cost of the failing state. Under these four states, the Qi nation is indeed in great peril."

The king pondered Zhong-Li's counsel. To the surprise of his courtiers, the king nodded in agreement, "Those are awakening words, and you have shown me the truth. You are hereby named as Duke Wu Yan, and shall become my new queen."

In the ensuing years, King Shuan relied on his new queen to help rule the country. The king ceased frivolous constructions, got rid of his concubines, fired corrupt courtiers and invited learned men to serve in his court; and, he designated a crown prince to secure the line of succession for the country.

Historians credited Zhong-Li Chun for engineering The Great Qi Reformation. Unfortunately for Zhong-Li Chun—Duke Wu Yan—people remembered her more for her physical defects than her accomplishments. Scholars coined the term "Mao Si Wu Yan" for her, which literally translates to "The Face Like Wu Yan," and is used to describe a very ugly woman.

23
THE THREE MOVES OF LADY MENG

"Emulate Mother Meng, Choose Your Environment" is a well-documented phrase from the famous Chinese elementary primer, The Three Character Classic "三字经 (San Zi Jing)." The phrase encompasses the story of Lady Meng, mother of Mencius, who is responsible for rearing and teaching her son and molding him into one of the greatest scholars in ancient China.

Widowed Madam Meng worked hard to raise her son properly. Initially, she moved to a quiet neighborhood near a graveyard, and Meng soon noted her son playing burial games with the neighborhood kids, they cried and prayed to the dead. She was not pleased, she did not want to raise a son that was devoted to the ritual of the dead.

She moved into the city and found a place near the marketplace. At the new home, Mencius learned about trading, marketing, and butchering animals. Again Lady Meng frowned, she did not want her son to become a merchant or a butcher.

This time she chose a home near a school, where Mencius learned the cultured behaviors of the scholars. Finally, Lady Meng was content with her choice of the neighborhood, and Mencius started his lessons on books.

One day, when she was working on the loom, Mencius came home early from school. He grumbled about the dull texts and said he was tired of studying, he thought it was a waste of time. Lady Meng took a shear and slashed the cloth she had woven on the loom. The violent act shocked the youth. "Why did you cut the cloth you worked so hard to weave?" He asked.

"The same reason you are tired of studying. To build anything, one must work hard. You need to study to acquire knowledge so that you can make something of yourself, and be a proper person."

"Studying is like weaving on the loom, you must work on it an inch at a time; you study daily to build up your knowledge. To quit studying is akin to taking a blade to the weaving, you sever your path to the future and ruin your life like this piece of cloth on the loom." With those words, she convinced Mencius to return to his studies.

Chinese scholars lauded her for being willing to endure hardship and sacrifice to rear her son properly. Two thousand and five hundred years after her passing, Chinese people still cite her as an example to encourage children to grow through education. Her legacy was Mencius, who became revered as the Saint of Scholars. He ranks only behind Confucius who was known as the God of Scholars.

24
THE ROAR OF THE HE-DONG LIONESS

*"The Gentleman of Long-Ciu is pious and bright,
learned and hospitable he debates into the night.
Then the He-Dong Lioness roars,
thus his staff tumbles and his mind crumbles."*

Su Dong-Poh, renowned poet of North Song Dynasty, China (960—1127AD)

Chen Ji-Chang, a well-learned scholar of the North Song Dynasty, lived in Long-Ciu city. His wife, Lady Liu, was beautiful but a shrew. Chen's scholarly repute was only overshadowed by his fear of his mate.

Chen was well respected for his profound knowledge of the Buddhist sutra and enjoyed debating the finer points of Buddhist scripture with his colleagues and often did so well into the night. However, Lady Liu did not share his appreciation for the scholarly gatherings that lasted long past darkness. When she decided it was time for his guests to leave, she banged the wall with a staff to shoo away Chen's guests.

One day, acting against his wife's wishes, Chen could not help himself and joined his friends in a prolonged social gathering in town. His friend, Su Dong-Poh accompanied Chen home that evening then departed when everything appeared tranquil. By happenstance, Su returned to discuss a scholarly point with his friend. As he crossed the threshold, he heard a loud crash from inside of the house. He rushed in only to find Chen cowering in a corner of the study with his staff, the source of the sound heard by Su, laid on the ground at Chen's side while Madam Liu boisterously berated the quivering scholar.

Su astutely retreated from the house, and on the way home composed a poem for his friend (as translated above). Su's literary renown quickly promoted "The Roar of the He-Dong Lioness" into a well-read poem, and the term "Lioness of He-Dong" became an aphorism used to describe a loud and overbearingly shrewd woman.

The 'Roar of the He-Dong Lioness' was an especially apt title because Chen was well respected for his studies in Buddhism. The 'Roar of the Lion' in Buddhist scripture represented the "Voice of the Holy Buddha," the spiritual prominence of that religion. In the case of his poem, Su Dong Poh used the term to refer to the shrill screams of Chen's wife. Lady Liu was from the He-Dong region east of the Yellow River, ergo the namesake of the 'He-Dong Lioness.'

Unfortunately for Master Chen Ji-Chang, the poem made him infamous throughout the Imperial realm, and 'Ji-Chang's Habit' became the literary term for describing a henpecked husband.

25
YEHENALA BUXIYAMALA, THE CALAMITY PRINCESS

Yehenala, also known as Dong Ge, was a Manchurian princess of the Ye He tribe. At her birth in 1582, the tribal shaman prophesized the young princess would either "build a nation, or destroy a nation." She was very beautiful and renowned as the prettiest woman of Manchuria.

In 1591, Lord Dai Shan, chief of the Ha Da tribe sought marriage with the nine-year-old Princess Dong Ge. Bo Zhai, Dong Ge's father and chief of the Ye He tribe consented, and invited Dai Shan to come and fetch the young bride. Unfortunately for Dai Shan, Bo Zhai ambushed and killed his expectant son-in-law and robbed the caravan. Suddenly, at the tender age of nine, Dong Ge became a widow. With the killing of Dai Shan, Bo Zhai gained influence and power and became the leader of the Alliance of Four Tribes in Manchuria.

At that time, the Wu La tribe was a rising power under the leadership of Lord Bu Zhan Tai with a following of five Manchu tribes. The Wu La was opposed by Nurhaci of the powerful Jurchen tribe at Jian Zhou. Bo Zhai promised Dong Ge to Bu Zhan Tai if he would join in the fight against Nurhaci. The combined force of nine tribes under Bo Zhai and Bu Zhan Tai attacked Jian Zhou but were defeated by Nurhaci. Bo Zhai died in battle and Bu Zhan Tai was captured and imprisoned by Nurhaci. Thus ended Dong Ge's second betrothal.

Bu Yang Gu, older brother of Dong Ge succeeded to be chief of the Ye He tribe. He promised Dong Ge to Nurhaci to secure the survival of his tribe. Impetuously, Dong Ge refused to marry the killer of her father; at the time Nurhaci was already married to Dong Ge's aunt. The young princess swore, "Nurhaci is the murderer of my father, I will marry whoever kills him!" Accordingly, the Ye He tribe rescinded the marriage contract of their princess to the Jurchen tribal chief.

Mong Geh Bu Lu, the new chief of the Ha Da tribe, responded to Dong Ge's declaration and signed the marriage agreement. In May 1599, Mong Geh Bu Lǚ declared war against Nurhaci. Unfortunately, Mong Geh Bu Lǚ was defeated, and the Ha Da tribe was wiped out by Nurhaci within two years.

Six years later, in 1607, Lord Bai Yin Da Li, leader of the Hui Fa tribe abandoned his marital vow with a daughter of Nurhaci then arranged a marriage with Dong Ge. The irate Nurhaci attacked and wiped out the Hui Fa people.

Meanwhile, Bu Zhan Tai, lord of the Wu La tribe had been released by Nurhaci after three years of imprisonment when he agreed to marry one of Nurhaci's daughters. However, the Wu La tribal chief could not forget his marriage vow to the beautiful Princess Dong Ge. In 1612, he reneged on his betrothal to the Jurchen princess (Nurhaci's daughter) and renewed his marriage vow to the Ye He princess. He then attacked the Jurchen tribe. Nurhaci responded with force and within two years wiped out the Wu La tribe. Bu Zhan Tai fled to Ye He territory and died soon afterward without consummating his marriage with Dong Ge.

By 1615, the thirty-three-year-old Princess Dong Ge had become an old spinster by local standards. Women of the time were usually married in their teens, became mothers before twenty and were grandmothers in their thirties. Prince Ghi Sai, son of the Eastern Mongol Yuan Tu tribal chief proposed marriage to Dong Ge. Bu Yang Gu, Dong Ge's brother, consented to the betrothal; however, the old virgin princess again nixed the arrangement. Meanwhile, two more suitors emerged on the scene, the once jilted Nurhaci, and Prince Meng Gu Er Dai, the son of Lord Dahl Khan, chief of the East Mongol Khalkha tribe. Once again, Bu Yang Gu (Dong Ge's brother), saw an opportunity to weaken Nurhaci's power. With Dong Ge's agreement, the seven-time betrothed Ye He princess finally became a bride (of Prince Meng Gu Er Dai). The twice jilted Nurhaci wanted to attack the Ye He but refrained because the Ye He tribe had allied with the Imperial Ming Empire. However, the Jurchen chief predicted, "That woman (Dong Ge) is cursed; the Ha Da, Hui Fa, and Wu La tribes had all been destroyed because of her. As Ye He stood with the Mongols against me, she will also bring doom upon that tribe (Ye He). As for Dong Ge, her days are numbered." Prophetically, Dong Ge died of illness, within a year after her marriage to the Mongol prince. Three years later, in August 1619, Nurhaci's army smashed the Ye He tribe to fulfill his prophecy.

Supposedly, before he died, Bu Yang Gu (Dong Ge's brother) made a counter-curse against the Jurchens, "So long as there is one Ye He woman alive, she will see to the destruction of the Jurchens." Ironically, in 1911, the

Dowager Empress Long Yu who signed the document for the abdication of the last Manchurian (Jurchen) Emperor Pu Yi was a Ye He princess who also bore the name of Yehenala.

26

CHEN YUAN-YUAN, THE DIRGE SIREN OF THE MING DYNASTY

Chen Yuan-Yuan (1623—1681) was the artistic name of Xing Yuan. She was a famous courtesan in the Jin-Ling (modern-day Nanjing) area renowned for her beauty and artistic skills in poetry, painting, singing, and dancing. She lived during an era of turmoil and indirectly contributed to the end of the Ming dynasty.

The populist rebellion of Li Zhi-Cheng threatened to topple the Imperial Ming Empire, at the same time the Jurchens of Manchuria were poised north of the Great Wall. The fragile state of affairs distressed Emperor Chong Zheng. Lady Tian, a favorite concubine of the emperor, sought to help the ruler relax by bringing a few beautiful women into the palace to entertain the frazzled head of state. She sent her brother Tian Wan to procure the women.

Chen Yuan-Yuan's beauty and fame got her selected to join the emperor's harem. Unfortunately, the emperor was too preoccupied with the problems of the state, so Chen never was summoned to meet the Son of Heaven. Tian Wan gladly brought Chen home and took her as his own concubine.

At the time, General Wu San-Gui commanded the army at San-Hai-Guan, the eastern terminus of the Great Wall that held the Manchus at bay. Rebel success at Xi'an in western China caused the emperor to summon Wu into the Capital at Beijing for an audience.

Tian Wan sought to establish a closer relationship with the powerful general and invited him to a banquet. At the gala, Tian had Chen perform her singing and dancing routines to entertain his guests. Her beauty and artistic skills mesmerized the general. Wu promised Tian the protection of his army if Tian would give Chen to the general, and Tian readily agreed to do so.

Soon after acceptance of Chen as a concubine, Wu was ordered to return to San-Hai-Guan to fend off the Manchu threat; leaving Chen at home in Beijing. Unfortunately, Li Zhi-Cheng's rebel army besieged and captured Beijing, and Emperor Chong Zheng hung himself.

Li Zhi-Cheng sent Wu a letter, threatening the lives of Wu's family in Beijing if Wu did not surrender to Li. Wu was contemplating submission to the rebel army until he learned from the messenger that Chen had been taken as a concubine by Liu Zhong-Ming, a general of Li's army. In a fit of jealous fury, General Wu opened the gates of San-Hai-Guan and invited the Manchu army in to fight Li's rebel army.

The combined force of Wu's army and the Manchus defeated Li; however, after his defeat, Li executed Wu's entire family of thirty-nine people, save for Chen.

Meanwhile, the Manchus decided not to return to Manchuria, they remained south of the Great Wall and vanquished the remnants of the Ming empire to create the Imperial Qing Dynasty.

Wu found and reunited with Chen Yuan-Yuan. The newly enthroned Qing Emperor Shun-Zhi bestowed Wu as King of Ping-Xi with Yunnan Province as his fief. Chen tried unsuccessfully to persuade Wu to join the Ming loyalists and fight the Manchus. When Wu refused, the dejected Chen Yuan-Yuan became a nun at the Huaguo Temple in Kunming. Historians cited Chen as the reason that Wu San-Gui opened the gates for the Manchus to enter China. Most historians blamed Wu for disloyalty, but some people blamed her for the demise of the Ming Dynasty; they preferred the rule of the bandit Li Zhi-Cheng over the Manchus.

Part III

The Book of Fables

27
THE WALL OF A DREAM

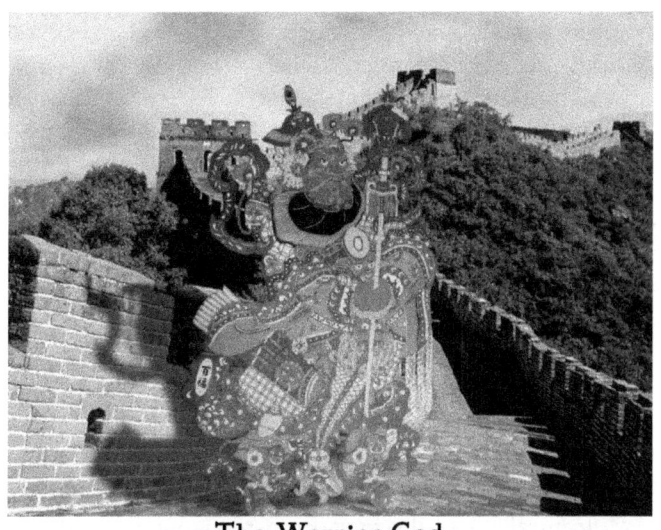

The Warrior God
But for a dream, the Great Wall was built; but for the wall, the empire fell.

He Zi-Qing
何自清, *Chinese historian*

In 214 BC, a giant red-faced warrior god visited the First Emperor of the Imperial Ch'in Empire in his dream. "Hu will be the one that destroys the Ch'in," the god warned. Perturbed, the superstitious emperor summoned the imperial astrologer for an interpretation. The astrologer declared "the god came to warn the emperor that the Hu people will destroy the Ch'in Empire." Hu was the name the Chinese called the northern nomads.

The emperor dispatched General Meng Tian with three hundred thousand men and drove the nomads away from northern China. Afterward, the general remained on the northern frontier to build the seven thousand and three hundred kilometers long Great Wall that stretched from Shan-Hai Guan on the Pacific coast to Jia-Yu Guan in the Gobi desert.

In 212 BC, Crown Prince Fu Su tried to dissuade the emperor from killing four-hundred and sixty alchemists and wizards. For his impertinence, the Emperor sent Fu Su to join Meng Tian in building the Great Wall. As a result, when the Emperor died in 210 BC, Fu Su was not around to assume the throne. It provided an opening for Prime Minister Li Shi and Senior Eunuch Zhao Gao to promote Prince **Hu** Hai to be the new Emperor.

Li Shi forged an imperial decree that ordered Fu Su to commit suicide, and the Crown Prince obediently slit his own throat.

Once in power, **Hu** Hai proved to be a cruel despot, he murdered all of his brothers and sisters. His repressive policies caused a revolt that brought down the Ch'in Empire, thus fulfilling the prophecy— "**Hu** will be the one that destroys the Ch'in."

Ironically, had the First Emperor ignored the dream there would have been no Great Wall, Fu Su would have inherited the throne and the Ch'in Dynasty would not have fallen.

28

THE VICTORY CHORUS

Victory without a battle is the pinnacle of strategy.
Sun Tzu, The Art of War

In 203 BC, Liu Bang fought Xiang Yu for control of China. Xiang Yu was a charismatic aristocrat while Liu Bang was a streetwise commoner. After six years of struggle, Liu managed to surround Xiang Yu and his fifty thousand men at Gai-Xia.

Liu had three hundred thousand men, but he was concerned that Xiang Yu might break out and escape to his home base—the Chu territory—east of the Yangtze River.

Liu Bang ordered his men to take singing lessons.

That night, Han soldiers serenaded their enemies with folk songs from the Chu territories, where Xiang Yu had recruited most of his troops. Their singing demoralized Xiang Yu and his men. It convinced the Chu general that Liu had already captured his (Xiang Yu's) homeland, and the majority of his men had surrendered to Liu Bang.

Despondent, the mightiest warrior of the land lost heart and gave up the fight. He dismissed his men to go home then wrote his own farewell poem while he drank wine with his favorite concubine:

Lament at Gai-Xia
> *Powerful as a mountain with ability higher than sky,*
> *Alas, time is not right and Zhui goes not forth.*
> *Zhui goes not forth and what could I do,*
> *Yu Ji oh Yu Ji what should I do (with thee).*
>> Xiang Yu, War Lord of Western Chu
>> *(Zhui was the name of Xiang Yu's war horse that he rode into battles, and Yu Ji was his concubine's name.)*

After Xiang Yu sang his poem, Yu Ji realized the end was near. She drew his sword and committed suicide to avoid abuse at the hands of the Han army. Tearfully, Xiang Yu buried Yu Ji then took the eight hundred men who chose to remain with him and rode south in a breakout attempt. They escaped undetected through the allied encirclements, but at dawn a five thousand man Han cavalry force was in hot pursuit. They caught up with Xiang Yu at the shore of the Wu River, and at the youthful age of thirty-one, the would-be emperor slit his own throat.

After Xiang Yu died, Liu Bang created the Imperial Han Dynasty and installed his former allies as kings. The name for the ethnic Han race of China originated from his dynasty. He was also the first of only two commoners to ever become the Emperor of China.

Xiang-Yu was a valiant warrior who won every battle except the last one. In this case, pragmatism and wiles triumphed over chivalry and righteousness. The Han army chorus line sang the dirge for Xiang Yu.

This is a rare occasion where an army won a battle with songs rather than swords.

29

THE PARABLE OF FORTUNES IN A HORSE LOST

Residing on the wide expanse of the grassy plains at the whim of nature gives Joe an acquiescent perspective on life. He has but one regret, heirs. Granted he has Jason, but the son of a poor farmer at the fringe of civilization has a hard time finding a wife. Joe pondered the matter then decided to buy an ox to work the farm. Perhaps, with the help of a draught animal, in time he would be able to save enough money for a proper dowry for his son to marry and produce heirs.

On market day, he went into town to buy a cow. Cows were prized for their durability, stability, and utility on the farm, and thus pricey. Joe soon realized he could not afford a cow, but he needed an animal to work the farm. So, he settled for a horse; actually, he got a mare.

Bewildered neighbors were surprised and amused. Why would a farmer want a horse? Of course, the horse could help till the land, but it was temperamental and took time away from chores to feed and maintain the animal. Joe and his horse became the talk of the village. Joe merely shrugged and went about his work.

One early morning, a noisy commotion brought Joe out of his hovel. Jason ran up with panted breath, "Father, father, our mare got out of the corral and ran off into the hills. I tried to find her but lost her trail in the grasslands." In an instant, Joe's dream of a dowry and heirs were scattered into the wind.

But Joe did not become upset, he merely shook his head in resignation, "It probably is for the best, it is a lot of work to maintain a horse. Don't fret over it; get back to work and make sure the rest of the animals don't follow that horse out of the barnyard."

Several neighbors came by to offer their sympathies. Wang, the village elder, noticed Joe was unfazed at having lost a valuable property. "My condolences for the loss of your horse," Wang said.

Joe gave a philosophical nod and shrugged his shoulders, "It is the will of the gods. My being upset will not bring the horse back. Look on the bright side, it means I will no longer have to cut as much hay and have no horse manure in the barn to shovel." The villagers were nonplussed at the eccentric reaction of their host and returned to their work.

A fortnight after, to the astonishment of all, the mare returned to Joe's home accompanied by a tall, graceful stallion. Everyone in the village came and admired the stallion and congratulated Joe on his good fortune. Once again, Wang noticed the lack of emotion in the man's matter-of-fact acceptance of the gift from Heaven. "Are you not happy with the return of your mare and the gaining of such a stallion?"

Joe shook his head and shrugged, "The mare came back because this is her home; however, to receive such a fine gift from the gods without any effort on my part is not necessarily a good happening. Who knows what could befall us in the future because of the arrival of the steed." The befuddled well-wishers politely nodded their heads and then scattered.

Jason adored the stallion. He fed the horse the finest grain and rode it frequently to show off his riding technique on the majestic steed. Everyone envied Joe's good fortune. Then, one day, the horse stumbled and threw its rider, who broke his leg in the fall. Once again, the neighbors congregated at Joe's home to offer sympathies, but Joe was philosophical over the accident. He calmly told the villagers, "Riding a horse is a dangerous affair; my son could have broken his neck and died. So a leg injury is not necessarily a bad outcome from the incident." Again, his neighbors shook their heads in bewilderment and then left.

In the following month, nomadic tribesmen invaded the region. All young men of the village were in the local militia and were summoned into the army; not one of them returned home from the war. Jason's leg injury precluded his entry into the army, and the unfortunate demise of the other young men of the village made him a very desirable commodity for the matchmaker.

Joe shook his head and his face finally cracked into a wistful grin. His intuition to buy an animal had been justified. It achieved the goal of getting Jason married, albeit in a roundabout way. Perhaps was it time to sell the stallion, it would not do to have Jason fall off the horse again. Besides, it would fetch some money to add a room for new additions to the family.

30
THE FISHERMAN'S CATCH

This episode gave birth to a well-known Chinese proverb. It cautions people from rash, aggressive acts without due consideration of the consequence—the embodiment of the Chinese philosophy that emphasizes peaceful coexistence.

Around 300 BC, a dozen feudal kingdoms divided the Yellow River basin, in the heartland of China. The Warring States Era had lived up to its name, with continuous conflicts flaring across the land.

The King of Zhao, one of the seven major powers, decided to attack his eastern neighbor, the Yen Kingdom. News of the war preparations and mobilization quickly spread through the populace and alerted the omnipresent spies. Within days, messengers delivered information regarding the impending invasion to the Yen court.

A prudent monarch, the King of Yen had no desire for senseless warfare, but neither did he wish to surrender his hereditary fief to the powerful Zhao Kingdom. He immediately ordered a mobilization of his army; at the same time, he held a council of war with his court advisors.

The hawkish Yen generals eagerly counseled to march the army to the western border, to meet the enemy on the field of honor. Zhao may have been bigger and more powerful, but the Yen nation had the advantage of shorter supply lines and familiarity of the terrain. Besides, Yen soldiers would fight with the moral cause of defending their homeland. The Yen generals argued for the honor of commanding the army, to send the invaders to a premature reunion with their ancestors in the afterlife.

During a pause in the presentation of the proposed war plan, Shu Dai, a minor minister, rose from his cushion and bowed to the King. "I agree that our valiant soldiers can defeat the invading Zhao army. However, it would cost us many lives and other resources, not to mention the disruption of the national economy. I would endeavor to meet the King of Zhao and attempt to persuade him to withdraw his army, without resorting to force."

The King lifted his jade scepter to silence the budding protests from his generals. "True," he said, "a military campaign would cost us much, even if we succeeded in defeating the enemy. And, as Sun Tzu, the military genius has told us, 'The best victory is one that is achieved without having to give battle.' We shall practice diplomacy before use of force. If you, Shu Dai, can persuade the Zhao ruler to turn back his army, it would be the same as if we had defeated it through the use of force, without the expenditure of lives and resources. And, if you should fail in your mission, we would still have the alternative of using the army to make the enemy see the errors of its ways. You have my permission to visit the Zhao court and see what you can do about warding off the invasion through diplomacy."

With a wave of his hand, the King dismissed Shu Dai and turned his attention to discuss details of the mobilization with his generals.

Shu Dai left the palace to summon his chariot and immediately traveled east toward the Zhao Kingdom. By diplomatic convention, in spite of the imminent state of war between the two countries, protocol demanded that Shu Dai was received with honor in the Zhao court. The King of Chao expected Shu Dai to bring tributes and plead for a negotiated peace. To intimidate Shu Dai, and gain a psychological advantage in the expected peace negotiation sessions, the King ordered Shu Dai's chariot be routed past the Zhao army cantonment. The resplendently armored soldiers paraded in formation to welcome the Yen emissary.

On arrival at the royal palace, Shu Dai endured a long wait while courtiers announced his presence to the King. The Yen emissary perceived the intended purpose of the King's maneuvers and used the time to plan his own strategy. Finally, a eunuch arrived to summon him to the Zhao court.

The King greeted without rising from his dais. "How was your trip here, honored Minister? Did you notice anything of interest along the way?"

Shu Dai knew the King referred to the marshaled Zhao troops that had lined the roads leading to the palace. The Yen envoy pointedly ignored the subject and made use of the opening to his own advantage. He bowed to the King then settled comfortably onto the cushion before venturing a response. "Thank you for your concern, great King. I had a very interesting trip. On my way, I saw something that was quite unique. I believe it merits relating before we get down to the real business at hand."

At a loss as to the direction of Shu Dai's conversation, the King nodded his head in polite agreement. "Oh, that is very considerate of you. Please enlighten us with your experience."

"I was riding along the Ie river, which, as you know, forms the border that divides our two nations. It so happened that I saw a giant freshwater clam sunning itself in the shallow waters, near the shore on the Yen side of the river. The clam had his shell wide open to bask in the sun's comforting warmth. Suddenly, a dark shadow blocked the sun's warm ray. Before the clam could notice any danger, a large crane darted across the sky from the Zhao side of the river and stabbed its long sharp beak into the clam's soft flesh. Reflexively, the surprised clam slammed its shell shut, trapping the crane's beak between the two halves of the shell.

"The crane danced and pulled, but no matter how hard the bird shook and struggled, it could not get its beak out of the trap. Nor could it fly off, due to the size and weight of the clam attached to its beak. After a while, the crane became exhausted and dizzy from struggling with the clam. The bird paused in his tussle and mumbled through its closed beak to the clam, 'If you don't let me go, you shall die of thirst in the hot sun.' The clam immediately snorted a retort. 'It is you who should let go first, otherwise, you will die of thirst and hunger, you greedy murderous fowl.' For good measure, it squirted a jet of water into the crane's eye and clamped its shell tighter.

"Since neither would agree to give in, they continued the impasse, each hoping the other would tire and give up. They remained thus in a standoff until a fisherman came downstream from the direction of the Ch'in land. The flapping of the crane's white feathery wings attracted the fisherman's attention. He pulled the boat closer and saw, near the edge of the water, the crane struggling with its beak stuck in the shell of a giant clam. The fisherman quickly beached his boat on the sandy bottom and, with a practiced toss of the net, captured the crane and the clam. The surprised combatants immediately released their grip on each other, but by then their fate had been sealed. With very little effort, the fisherman had a good harvest that day. Does it really matter if either the crane or the clam went into the fisherman's pot a little sooner than the other?

"That was the end of the crane and the clam. Now, today, we have the Zhao and the Yen Kingdoms, two neighbors ready to fight each other to the death, like the crane and the clam. In the end, when the two sides are exhausted from the fight, the Kingdom of Ch'in, Your

Majesty's western neighbor, shall play the role of the fisherman and come in to reap his harvest. Therefore, I urge you, great King. Consider well, before you decide to launch your army toward the Yen border."

The King mulled over Shu Dai's words and realized the danger of invading the Kingdom of Yen with the powerful Ch'in Kingdom poised at his rear.

"You are so right," he said. "Was it not for your wise counsel, both our nations would be served up as the Ch'in's next morsels. You may return and tell your master that the Zhao army will not march into the Yen Kingdom."

31
GOOD WILL

Mong-Tsang Chun is a name commonly used by Chinese to describe an exceptionally generous person. The original Mong-Tsang Chun, the Duke of Mong-Tsang, served as the First Minister of the Qi nation during the Era of the Warring Nations, at around 300 B.C. He kept as many as three thousand houseguests at his palatial estate. They came from all levels of society and usually possessed special skills or knowledge. Mong-Tsang Chun owed much of his fame and diplomatic successes to this legion. This story concerns the Duke and one of his "houseguests."

In the city of Lin Tzu, the Capital of the Qi Kingdom, a stranger arrived at the First Minister's mansion and requested to see the Duke of Mong-Tsang. The visitor wore rough cotton clothing, straw sandals, and carried an unsheathed sword at his waist. The gate guards, used to the coming and going of strange visitors, did not turn the man away.

Mong-Tsang Chun welcomed the stranger with the respect and honor due an equal. "Thank you for honoring me with your visit. Is there anything particular you wish to discuss with me?"

"No, not particularly, I have heard that you like to befriend people, regardless of their background. I, therefore, decided to offer my services to you."

"Do you have any special skills or knowledge to enlighten me?"

"Nothing really that is worth mentioning."

"Is there then, anything special you wish to ask me?"

"Not really, except that I would like to be one of your houseguests." Impressed with the man's audacity and forthrightness, Mong-Tsang Chun gave Fong Huan a room in the third rank guest facility.

Ten days later, Mong-Tsang Chun summoned the manager of the guest facilities. "How is our new guest doing?"

The manager sighed in frustration and shook his head in bewilderment. "Master Fong appears to have been destitute before his arrival at our door. He came with no personal items, other than a sword, which he dangles on his waist with a hemp cord. There wasn't even a sheath for that piece of tin. However, if nothing else, the man is not afraid to speak his mind. At the evening of each day, he beats a tune on his sword and sings, 'Oh dear sword, let's go home, for there is no meat with our meals."

Mong-Tsang Chun chuckled at the news, "I suppose he is complaining that I have been a stingy host. Move him to the second rank guest facility and report to me in five days."

In due time, the Manager reported, "Master, our guest, Mr. Fong, is still singing, but this time he sings a different tune. Now he sings 'Oh dear sword, let's go home, for there is no carriage for us to ride in."

"Amazing, the man thinks he should be ranked among the elite of my houseguests. He must have some yet-undiscovered talent to boast of such self-confidence. Move him to the top rank facility and let me know what music he makes there."

A few days later, Mong Tsang Chun was again surprised by the report he received. "Each day, Master Fong Huan leaves the compound early in the morning and returns after dark. No one knows where he goes or what he does. When he is about, one can hear him beating the same tune on the sword and singing 'Oh dear sword, let's go home, for we have no one we can come home to."

Mong-Tsang Chun shook his head and laughed in exasperation, "Is there no end to the man's appetite? We'll see how far he will go with our hospitality. Buy a wife for him to keep him warm at night."

Finally, Fong Huan ceased his musical renditions and tranquility reigned.

One day, the overseer of the manor requested an audience with Mong-Tsang Chun. "Master, we have only enough money to run the estate for another month." Faced with a financial shortage, Mong-Tsang Chun called a meeting of his household staff.

"We are running short of money. Who should I send to collect interest on loans I provided to the people of Hsueh?"

The Manager of the guest facilities suggested. "Remember our singing guest, Master Fong? I have not been able to discern any special talent in him. But, he seems honest enough to be trusted with this task. Besides, he has promoted himself to the top rank. It would be a good opportunity to test his true worth."

Mong-Tsang Chun nodded and sent for Fong Huan. "We are running short of operating funds. I had made loans to the people of Hsueh. Now I need someone to collect money from the borrowers. Would you like to do this job?"

"As you wish, sir. However, after collecting the money, is there anything special that you wish for me to acquire before I return to Lin Tzu?"

Mong-Tsang Chun paused to ponder the question. He glanced over at his staff, and received a round of headshakes and shrugged shoulders. "Use your judgment and buy whatever you think I need."

Fong Huan arrived at Hsueh city, the ancestral fief of Mong-Tsang Chun. He settled into the local magistrate's residence and sent word for all the people who had borrowed money from the Duke of Mong-Tsang to come and pay off their loans. Most of the city's over 10,000 households had borrowed money from their Duke. Within a few days, Fong Huan collected a substantial sum, but a large number of the loans were still outstanding. On the fourth day, when no more people showed up to pay off their loans, Fong Huan sent messengers to announce throughout the city: "All people with outstanding loans are invited to attend a large banquet at the magistrate's residence, regardless of their ability to repay the loan. They are also to bring their loan contracts for validation."

Enticed by free food and drinks, all the borrowers appeared for the banquet. Fong Huan encouraged everyone to eat and drink. At the end of the banquet, Fong Huan took out his copies of the loan agreements and proceeded to match them with those being held by individual borrowers. For those people that he felt were financially capable of carrying the loan, Fong Huan extended the terms of their loans, to be paid with interest at a later date. As Fong Huan turned to deal with the other borrowers - those who were too poor to make even interest payments - they knelt en masse, in front of Fong Huan and begged to be granted extensions on their loans also.

To the surprise of everyone present, Fong torched the remaining loan documents. As the loan contracts burned into ashes, he turned to the gaping guests. "The reason that the Duke of Mong-Tsang loaned money to you was to make sure that you were able to live decently. He did not intend to get rich off of you. However, the Duke has a large estate and keeps thousands of houseguests like myself, which requires large sums of money to feed and clothe them. That is why he needs to collect money on your loans. Today, according to the Duke's instructions, I have extended the loans for those who are able to pay the interest. At the same time, I have burned the loan contracts of those who are too poor to pay back the loan. All of you must appreciate the benevolence of our Duke, Mong-Tsang Chun." He then entered the carriage, amidst thundering cheers from the populace, for the return trip to Lin Tzu.

By the time Fong Huan returned to the Capital, reports of his deeds at Hsueh had preceded him to Mong-Tsang Chun's ear. The Duke was not pleased. When Fong Huan arrived to report on the trip, Mong-Tsang Chun politely inquired about his health before venturing into the business at hand. "Master Fong, thank you for laboring on my behalf. Did you have a nice trip?"

"Yes master, the weather was fine and I encountered no problem in the accomplishment of my task."

"Did you collect on all of the debts owed to me at Hsueh?"

"Yes sir, I not only collected the debts, but I also collected good will for you."

Mong-Tsang Chun could no longer contain his temper. He retorted angrily. "I have three thousand houseguests and am short of funds to feed and clothe them. That was why I loaned money to the people of Hsueh, to supplement my needs at the manor. You feasted the loan holders, burned half of the outstanding loan contracts. Now you say you collected good will. What good will do you refer to, and how can it be of benefit to me?"

Fong Huan remained nonplused. "Master, please be patient and calm down and let me explain. There were a lot of people from whom I was unable to collect money on the loans. If I hadn't used the banquet as an enticement, chances were that very few people would have shown up to meet with me. I could not track down each and every one of the delinquent borrowers, not to mention properly assess their abilities to repay the loans. At the banquet, I was able to judge and segregate those that could from those that could not pay back their loans.

"By extending loans to those that were able to pay, I ensured your ability to collect on those debts at a future date. The ones that were too poor, I forgave their loans because they would not have been able to repay their loans no matter how hard they were pressed. In time the interest on their loans would have been so high that they would move away from Hsueh city, just to escape their debts. Hsueh is your hereditary fief, its people are your base of support. Today, I burned the loan contracts to show them you value the people more than you value their gold. Your reputation for justice and kindness shall spread far and wide." He then paused to add with emphasis. "That is what I meant by collecting good will. Before I left for Hsueh, you told me to buy what I thought was lacking here. Well, I felt you could do with some good will."

Mong-Tsang Chun was skeptical of the value of Fong Huan's deed, but what was done could not be undone, so he let it pass and kept Fong Huan as his house guest.

The Qi nation prospered and gained influence under the stewardship of the Duke. A powerful Qi did not bode well for the neighboring Ch'in Kingdom. The King of Ch'in sent spies to spread rumors to malign Mong-Tsang Chun. The King of Chi, duped by malicious rumors, fired the Duke from his job of the Prime Minister. As the proverb said—When a tall tree falls, the resident monkeys scatter away. Mong-Tsang Chun's houseguests left him like rats abandoning a ship on fire. Only Fong Huan remained loyal to serve his benefactor.

Fong Huan drove Mong-Tsang Chun in his carriage to Hsueh. Miles outside of the Hsueh city limit, the people of

Hsueh, bearing food and refreshments, lined the road to welcome their Duke. Mong Tsang Chun was moved to tears by the warmth and ardor of the populace. At length, he turned to Fong Huan and bowed. "Thank you, Master Fong, I have just now learned the value of collecting the good will of the people."

Within in a year, Fong Huan helped the Duke return to power in the Qi Court.

32
CHOU CHU AND THE THREE GREAT EVILS

The Chinese, like the people in every other country of the world, admire heroes. This is the story of Chou Chu, an unwitting non-hero.

Chou Chu, a tall strapping young man, was the only son of a wealthy merchant. Chou Chu's parents aspired to have their son achieve fame and honor as an official at the Emperor's Court. Even as Chou Chu was a small child, his father hired scholars to train him in Confucian philosophy and other literary subjects.

But Chou Chu had other interests. He preferred swordplay over poetry and classics. Learned scholars are one copper piece to the dozen, and they usually remain nameless figures in history, whereas successful generals win eternal glory, with riches and honors that are the envy of Gods. Chou Chu was happiest when he practiced martial arts. His sturdy frame and immense strength provided an excellent foundation for physical endeavors. Chou Chu's devotion to martial skills earned accolades from his Kung

Fu masters but elicited great despair among his scholarly mentors. In frustration, his academic tutor resigned, followed by a score of other replacements, none of whom lasted more than one month; thereafter, no scholar in the district would accept a teaching position in the Chou manor. This of course, only made Chou Chu happier, because it allowed more time for martial arts! Reluctantly, Chou Chu's parents abandoned their lofty hopes for the young man.

Chou Chu's second passion involved practical jokes and mischief. Not a day passed without some villager grumbling about Chou Chu's pranks. When Grandmother Li asked Chou Chu to pick some apples from a tree, he pulled out the whole tree by the roots. When Farmer Wang searched for a stray ox, Chou Chu brought the ox back on his shoulders and deposited it on the roof of the farmer's house. The villagers were angry, but because of his strength and martial arts skill, they were afraid to take him to task. Besides, Chou Chu's father was a model citizen of the village. One should always consider the master before punishing his dog.

One day, Chou Chu came upon a little girl sitting at the end of the bridge leading to the village square, large tears streaming down her cheeks. Curious, Chou Chu stopped and knelt next to the little girl, "Oh, little sister, why are you crying?"

The girl sniffled, wiped her tears with a small handkerchief then looked up at the tall youth. "I grew up in this village and all my friends are here. Now my father says we will have to move to another village. This means I will have to leave all my friends and never see them again." She lowered her head and resumed sobbing.

"Why do you have to move away from our village?"

"Because there are three great evils threatening the people of this village. My father fears for our safety."

A surge of bravado coursed through Chou Chu's torso and he puffed up his chest. "How is it that no one told me about these three evils? I would have destroyed them for the village. Tell me, what are these three great evils and where are they? I will remove them for you so that you won't have to leave your home."

The little girl paused in her sniffling and looked doubtfully at Chou Chu. Chou Chu straightened his six-foot frame. "Look, little sister, I am a master of the martial arts. I can jump to the top of a tree in one leap, catch a bird with my bare hands and return to the ground before you can count from one to three. See!" And he leaped up into the tree, then returned, landing with a smile and a chirping bird in his grasp.

The feat stemmed the flow of tears and the look of admiration pouring from the little girl's eyes shot glowing warmth through Chou Chu's veins. "Now tell me about those three great evils of yours," Chou Chu said as he sat down beside the child to better savor her admiration.

The girl paused to catch her breath, then glanced over up at her hero. "There is a large tiger in the southern mountains. It has already eaten three villagers in the past week. Now everyone is afraid to go into the mountains to gather firewood."

Chou Chu smiled nonchalantly, "I'm not afraid of tigers. I'll go and kill him tomorrow. Meet me in the village square two days from now, and I will give you the tiger skin as a present."

Chou Chu then marched home to prepare for the next morning's tiger hunt. He told no one of his plans, but quietly honed and polished his sword and spear. Early the next morning, he prepared a big sack of juicy stewed meat and steamed bread, and started down the road to the southern mountains.

Chou Chu, although a skilled fighter, had no experience as a hunter. He spent the entire morning and most of the afternoon stomping through the woods, climbing from one hilltop to another, searching for the tiger. He did not know that tigers disliked the daytime heat; instead, they hunted in the evening coolness. Chou Chu's thrashing in the woods only succeeded in scaring the tigers away. As the sun descended into the western horizon, the darkness advanced and overtook the forest. Chou Chu grew weary and irritated at his inability to make good his promise to the little girl. With a sigh of disappointment, Chou Chu decided to find some water and prepare to spend the night in the mountains. His pride would not allow him to return and face the little girl empty-handed. At a soft grassy spot by a stream, he stopped to make camp.

Chou Chu drew the sword from his waistband and laid it along with the spear under a willow tree near the stream. He knelt and slurped thirstily from the cool mountain stream, allowing the refreshing water to wash the day's frustration from his face and mind. He then rose and untied the bundle of food he had carried on his back. Suddenly, a mountain breeze brought a whiff of feral odor. Chou Chu spun around to face two fist-sized golden orbs peering at him from the tall grass at the edge of the clearing. Chou Chu's hand touched his side and he realized he had moved out of reach of his weapons and there was no time to search for them.

With a throaty growl that quickly turned into a fierce roar, a giant, long sinewy shape burst out of the darkness toward Chou Chu. He instinctively tucked his chin into his chest and rolled to one side, landing in a perfect bow stance - left foot in front of the right.

Chou Chu knew he had finally found the tiger, or rather, the tiger had found him. The big worm—northern Chinese call the tiger as a big worm because of its black and gold stripes--landed with a thud and tried to sweep its prey off balance with body and tail. Chou Chu quickly leaped back, out of the way. Missing with its first two strikes, the enraged tiger gave a great roar, intending to frighten his victim into immobility. Chou Chu's martial art skills kicked into high gear and he roared back at the tiger as he went on the attack. With a snap of his wrist, Chou Chu hurled the only handy item, his food pouch, straight at the tiger's head.

The tiger reflexively snapped at the bundle and caught a mouth full of the fabric pouch. The tiger tasted flavored meat as its teeth pierced the cloth. While its jaws were clamped about Chou Chu's dinner, Chou Chu took two quick steps and leaped astride the tiger's back. He grasped a handful of skin on the tiger's nape with his left hand, while his right fist started pounding its head. The tiger, surprised by the sudden attack, could not get rid of the bundle that was entangled in his teeth. Between Chou Chu's fists pounding on his head and the choking bundle of food in his mouth, the tiger became frightened and tried to escape. But, it could not shake the rider off its back, nor breathe through the meat sauce-soaked cloth material, which had now wrapped itself over the tiger's nostrils.

Chou Chu felt the tiger weakening and he clamped his legs tighter around the beast's body while raining blows on its head with both fists. The tiger jumped and rolled on the ground, but Chou Chu locked his arms around its neck and started to choke the tiger. With a final spasm, the tiger collapsed on the grass. Blood flowed from its eyes, nose, ears, and mouth.

As the tiger stopped struggling, Chou Chu delivered one more punch and then rolled off the beast. He crawled over to his weapons and returned to finish the job. After a third thrust of the spear, with legs of tofu and trembling hands, Chou Chu collapsed into an exhausted slumber.

The next morning, he awoke to numbing pain in his bruised and swollen fists. The smell of blood and death startled him, and he realized that he had spent the night atop the dead tiger. It brought back the memory of the night's struggle. Moaning in pain, Chou Chu rolled off the tiger and stumbled into the stream. A long soak in the cool mountain water revived his battered body and washed the stink of death from his nostrils.

Chou Chu waded ashore and stripped off his torn, wet clothing. He built a fire for warmth, and to dry his clothing.

A rumble in his belly reminded him that the tiger had ruined his dinner during the fight. With a sardonic smile at the poetic justice, he cut a piece of meat from the tiger's haunch for breakfast. While the meat roasted over the fire, Chou Chu skinned the tiger. After the meal, he tied the pelt into a bundle, slung it over the end of his spear, and then started for the village.

Chou Chu marched proudly into the village square, smugly ignoring questioning looks from the villagers. At the temple in the center of the square, Chou Chu found the little girl waiting for him. Chou Chu placed the tiger skin at the little girl's feet. "I am sorry for keeping you waiting little sister, but this big worm was playing hide and seek with me in the mountains. I finally caught up with him last night, so here's your first great evil. It will never harm anyone again. Now, what is that second great evil of yours?"

The little girl caressed the tiger skin at her feet, admiration glowing on her face. "I am glad you are alive and well. For a while, I thought perhaps the big worm had gotten you also. Thank you for the gift of its skin."

She paused for breath and stroked the stiff fur on the tiger's head. "The second evil is a big black dragon in the river. It has been sinking village fishing boats and our fishermen are afraid to go out and catch fish from the river."

"We shall see how mean this river snake of yours can be," Chou Chu nodded a farewell to the girl, then walked to the village market and purchased an old cow. He stopped by his home to pick up his bow and arrows, and a large spear. The spear had a two-foot-long blade atop a ten-foot-long shaft and the diameter of a rice bowl. With the butt of his spear, Chou Chu drove the cow into the river, while he followed in a small sampan.

Suddenly, near the middle of the river, the cow bawled, and seemed to fly out of the water and into the air. When the air cleared, it became clear that the cow had been lifted completely out of the water in the maw of a black-scaled shiny dragon.

Before the dragon could sink back into the water, Chou Chu notched and fired two arrows. The missiles flew true, burying into the twin bulging, red lantern-like eyes behind the dragon's snout. The suddenly blinded dragon raised its head and roared in pain.

Chou Chu launched his long spear, piercing the body of the cow and pinning it against the roof of the dragon's palate. The dragon shook its head in pain and anger then rose into the sky before smashing its long thick body into the river surface. The impact sent towering waves rolling toward the shore. Chou Chu held on tightly to the rudder of the sampan and steered for a rocky crag on the riverbank.

He beached the sampan and leaped ashore then cupped his hands to shout at the dragon. "Come and get me, you big black snake, I am the one that took away your sight." Chou Chu continued shouting while sending one arrow after another toward the dragon's head.

The sightless dragon was in great pain and reacted instinctively to Chou Chu's taunts and arrows. Again and again, the giant serpentine body arched high into the air to smash down on the river surface, trying to crush its tormentor. The dragon's giant stag-horned head swung from side to side, trying to pinpoint Chou Chu's location via his voice. Suddenly, the beast roared and lunged at the spot where it believed its attacker to be. By the time the dragon's head landed on the spot, Chou Chu had already skipped away and the dragon smashed onto the jagged rocks on the shore. The force of the strike caused its fangs to slice the cow in its mouth into three sections; at the same time, the spear was driven through the roof of the dragon's snout, to shoot into the sky.

While the dragon was stunned by the collision, Chou Chu dropped his bow, leaped into the air and came down with the spear that he had caught in midair. With a slight pop, the spear penetrated the scale on the dragon's nape and pinned its head into the ground. With the head immobilized, the dragon had only its tail to use as a weapon. It swept the tail left and right smashing rocks, trees, boats and everything within its reach. Finally, the dragon curled and wrapped its body around a half smashed pine tree. Chou Chu easily dodged the flailing tail and, during a lull in the painful spasms, leaped forward with his sword drawn.

In two quick swings of his long blade, he chopped off the pair of stag horns that had adorned the dragon's head. The dehorned dragon quivered violently, then transformed into a large silver and black water snake, which fell quickly under Chou Chu's blade.

Chou Chu took the pair of dragon horns to the little girl, who had joined the crowd at the riverbank. Panting with sweat-covered pride, he handed her the pair of three foot long trophies. "Here is what's left of the second great evil. Now, what is that last great evil thing of the village? I cannot imagine anything that's stronger and more dangerous than those first two evils."

The little girl wrapped the dragon horns in the tiger skin then beamed proudly at her hero. "My father said that the last great evil is the village bully named Chou Chu. He is strong and a master of the martial arts. Everybody is afraid of him and his mischief. People can avoid the first two evils by staying away from the mountains and the river, but they must live in the village, where the third great evil also resides. He is the one that's really making life miserable for everyone in the village."

By then, the entire village had heard of Chou Chu's exploits against the big worm and had seen him battle the dragon. Now, they gathered about the little girl to hear the latest details. They were glad to see that Chou Chu had eliminated the second great evil, but some of them appeared disappointed that Chou Chu had not died with the evil dragon. Everyone was amused at the little girl's naming of their third great evil. They waited with anticipation to hear

Chou Chu's response. Some even feared for the little girl's safety.

The identity of the third great evil stunned and embarrassed Chou Chu. Perplexed at the sudden silence from her otherwise garrulous hero, the little girl looked up and tugged at Chou Chu's sleeve. "What's the matter? Are you afraid of Chou Chu also?"

Chou Chu mumbled in embarrassment. "No, little sister, I'm not at all afraid of Chou Chu. You see, I am Chou Chu, the third and final great evil of this village." He then raised his voice for all to hear. "I promise you, from this day onward, the third great evil shall cease to exist in this village. Tomorrow, Chou Chu will go into the provincial capital and enlist in the army. He will use his martial skills to fight the enemies of the realm, so as to atone for his past sins to the people of this village."

He then turned to the little girl. "And your family will not have to leave this village because all three great evils will have been eliminated." And, with those words, he turned and walked off without a sideward glance.

That evening, an assembly of elders gathered at the home of the village chief. The spokesman for the group rose from his seat and bowed to their host. "Master Lin, we have come to thank you on behalf of the entire village. Everything turned out beyond our best expectations. We are rid of the mountain tiger and the river dragon, while Chou Chu will be leaving tomorrow for the army."

The village chief stroked his long flowing beard while he nodded a contented smile. "It is a shame that Chou Chu must leave the village, but I think it is for the best that we let him go. He may have the best of intentions to change his behavior for the better, but as the proverb says 'It is easier to move a mountain than to change a person's character.'

"Besides, it would be difficult for everyone to keep our scheme a secret. I think it is best for all concerned that we allow him to visit his mischief on the Emperor's army and the nomadic barbarians." He then pointed with his folded fan toward an ornate chest in the corner of the room. "I shall keep the tiger skin and the dragon's horns as part of Fu Hsing's dowry."

"Yes, your granddaughter performed marvelously in baiting Chou Chu into your scheme. There will be a long line of matchmakers waiting to arrange a marriage for such an intelligent girl."

33
LIFE IN SEVEN PACES

This anecdote is the true account of the origin of a short but very famous poem in Chinese history. It lauds the virtues of poise and intelligence under stress.

Around 220 A.D., Cao Cao ruled China in the name of the Han Emperor. A renowned villain of the fabled Era of the Three Kingdoms (220-280 A.D.), he was the Chinese counterpart to Machiavelli and Bismarck. After Cao Cao died, his son Cao Pei ascended to the throne of the Wei Kingdom. Cao Pei felt his position threatened by his younger brother, the very popular Prince Cao Tze, who was renowned for his poetic artistry.

One day, Cao Pei devised a solution to the perceived threat against his throne. In the presence of all courtiers, the King summoned his brother to the fore and decreed, "You are supposedly a well-trained scholar, regarded as the best poet of the land. I want you to prove the veracity of your fame. You will give me a poem within the time of walking seven steps. Fail me and you earn an appointment with the Imperial Executioner. Now, start walking."

Before the other courtiers had recovered from the bizarre decree, Cao Tze started walking, and immediately began to deliver his epic creation—

The Seven Steps Verse.

煮豆燃豆萁	zhju dou ran dou gi
豆在釜中泣	dou zai fu zhong qi
本是同根生	ben shi tong gen sheng
相煎何太急	xiang jian he tai ji

The poem loosely translates to:
BEANSTALKS FEED THE FIRE
BEANS WEEP IN THE FRYER
WE'RE OF THE SAME ROOT
WHY FRY US IN SUCH HASTE

The short verse satisfied the Imperial decree while addressing the circumstance of the poem's creation, which only highlighted the genius the poet. Frustrated and embarrassed by the underlying connotation of the short verse, the King gave up on his attempt at fratricide.

34
THE PRICE OF HONOR AND INTEGRITY

Chinese people study the past to guide their future. The Court Historian has the important duty of recording all events in the realm for posterity. The post of the Historian is traditionally given to a respected scholar of impeccable honor and integrity.

In 547 B.C., Marquis Tsuang, a tyrannical despot, ruled the Qi Kingdom in northeastern China. He seduced the wife of his Minister Ts'ui Chu. In retaliation, Ts'ui Chu murdered the Marquis and installed Prince Ju Jiu as the new Marquis. The new ruler reciprocated by promoting Ts'ui Chu to the position of Prime Minister.

Ts'ui Chu demanded all Qi courtiers to swear a loyalty oath to the new regime. He then ordered Boh, the Court Historian, to record that Marquis Tsuang died of hepatitis.

Instead of obeying the order, Boh carved on the bamboo strip "In the summer month of May, on the Yi-Hai year, Ts'ui Chu assassinated his Lord Guang." The Prime

Minister read the newly inscribed strip and immediately put Boh to death. He then summoned Boh's three brothers, who were also Court Historians. Over the severed body of Boh, the Prime Minister ordered Chung, the senior of the three surviving brothers, to record anew the circumstance of the Marquis Tsuang's death.

Chung took out a strip from his sleeve and carved "In the summer month of May, on the Yi-Hai year, Ts'ui Chu assassinated his Lord Guang." Immediately, he too lost his head. Ts'ui Chu then turned to Shu, the next brother, and made the same demand; Shu followed Boh and Chung's examples and received the third execution order.

Over the three dead bodies, Ts'ui Chu waved three identically inscribed strips at Gi, the last of the brothers "You are the last of your clan. Do you not wish to live and continue your line? If you alter the record, I'll spare your life."

"Inscribe the truth, which is the duty of the Historian. To shy from one's duty so as to save one's only life is to live without honor, a fate worse than death. If I do not record the truth, the truth shall be carved by some other person under the Heaven. Inscribing falsehood shall not be sufficient to cover the shameful deed of the Prime Minister. It would only invite derision and ridicule from the people. I have no death wish, but will not part from duty and integrity. My life is in your hands."

The Prime Minister gave a rueful sigh "I did what I did for the good of the country. I had no choice in my deed. Go ahead and keep your truthfulness. People will understand the motive of my deeds." With that, he threw the bamboo strips at Gi. Gi sobbed as he gathered up his brothers' final testaments and left the palace.

At the palace gate, Gi encountered Master Nan Shi, another Court Historian. Nan Shi said "I had heard that your brothers were killed, and was afraid that no one would be left to record the May Yi-Hai incident. So I came with a bamboo strip to do my duty."

Gi opened his palm and displayed the three blood-stained epitaphs of his brothers.

Within one year, Ts'ui Chu himself died a violent death in a power struggle within the Qi Court.

35
DUAN WU, THE FIFTH OF MAY DRAGON BOAT FESTIVAL

The fifth of May in the Lunar Calendar is one of the oldest traditional holidays in the Chinese culture. It commemorates the passing of the greatest poet in ancient China—Qu Yuan (340-278 B.C.). He was the first man in Chinese history to be identified with a famous poem. With his epic poem "Li Sao" he created a new form of poetry aptly known as the "Sao" style. The "Sao" format of varying lengths allowed the creation of poems with more rhythm and flexibility. His artistic influence reached many later poets, to include Li Bai, the most celebrated of all Chinese poets. However, Qu Yuan was best known to the Chinese as a fervent patriot who gave his life for his country. Many people considered him as the founder of classical Chinese poetry.

A distant cousin of King Huai of the Chu Kingdom, Qu Yuan served as the senior minister and confidant of the ruler. He was loyal, intelligent and forthright. He helped build the kingdom into a powerful nation and pushed for the formation of an alliance with neighboring kingdoms to counter the powerful Ch'in Kingdom. However, his diplomatic success incurred the jealousy of his colleagues within the royal court and the enmity of the Ch'in court.

Qu Yuan successfully negotiated an alliance with five other kingdoms of the land to counter the Ch'in threat. This caused grave concern in the Ch'in Court at Xian-Yang. King Tso Hsiang of the Ch'in Kingdom felt that Qu Yuan held the key to weakening the Chu Kingdom and its alliances. The King of Ch'in sent his Prime Minister Zhang Yi to the Chu Court at Ying.

Zhang Yi first presented a pair of valuable jade stones to Queen Zheng Xiu, in return for her assistance in ousting Qu Yuan. Zhang Yi then offered six hundred lis (about one hundred miles) of land to King Huai, if he would commit to an alliance with the Ch'in Kingdom.

The King gleefully related the land offer to his wife. Queen Zheng Xiu said, "I am very happy that the Ch'in would cede so much land for an alliance with us. However, you should be aware that Qu Yuan had demanded a pair of fine jade stones from Zhang Yi, but was rebuffed by the Ch'in envoy. So, he would probably argue against the peace offer from the Ch'in."

The next day, as expected, Qu Yuan vehemently protested against a coalition with the Ch'in Kingdom. His violent objection prompted the King to fire his cousin and banished him from the royal court. With Qu Yuan out of the way, the anti-Ch'in alliance fell apart. Adding insult to injury, when King Huai tried to occupy the six hundred lis of land promised in the agreement, he was told by Zhang Yi that it was a misunderstanding—the Ch'in promised only six lis of land, not six hundred lis. In the ensuing conflict, the Chu army lost eighty thousand men, and seventy odd officers captured by the enemy, in addition to eight cities.

King Huai recalled Qu Yuan to repair the old anti-Ch'in alliance. However, the King could not resist a new peace proposal from the Ch'in Kingdom. This time, the Ch'in offered the return of half of the captured land, a beautiful courtesan, and a military alliance.

Qu Yuan was at the Qi Kingdom negotiating a military coalition. He rushed backed to the Chu Court and warned that the parley at Wu-Guan—outside of the Chu territory—was a plot, but his petition fell on deaf ears. Prince Tze Lan, the youngest son of the King, had married a Ch'in Princess and thus had a personal interest in a friendly relationship with his wife's homeland. He argued for attending the parley at Wu-Guan.

At Wu-Guan, General Bai Chi, the Ch'in Duke of Wu-An, took King Huai captive and brought him to Xian-Yang as a hostage for negotiations. King Huai refused to negotiate his own release and spent three years in captivity in the Ch'in Kingdom until his demise in 296 BC.

King Huai's eldest son had assumed the throne as King Qin Hsiang, who appointed his youngest brother Prince Tze Lan as a senior advisor. Qu Yuan vehemently criticized Prince Tze Lan because he had been instrumental in persuading King Huai to attend the parley at Wu-Guan. In retaliation, Prince Tze Lan accused Qu Yuan of having personal ambitions for the throne. The new King considered Qu Yuan as a holdover from the previous regime and, as a royal kinsman, a potential threat. Besides, King Qin Hsiang refused to undermine the position of his newly appointed senior advisor. It would be a sign of weakness that the new King could not afford. Ultimately, for a second time, Qu Yuan left the Chu royal court in disgrace.

In 278 B.C., General Bai Qi led the Ch'in army that invaded and sacked Ying, the capital of the Chu Kingdom.

King Qin Hsiang was forced to flee from the Capital. News of the military disaster drove Qu Yuan into a fit of frustration and despair. In a moment of depression, Qu Yuan threw himself into the Mi-Luo River.

The people loved and respected Qu Yuan for his patriotism and integrity. They immediately marshaled the boats for a rescue attempt. Alas, all efforts to save the courtier failed, people could not even recover his body. In desperation, people wrapped food in bamboo leaves and threw them into the Mi-Lou River to feed the fish, so that they would not touch Qu Yuan's body. They beat drums and gongs to scare evil spirits away from the body of the martyred poet.

Thereafter, the people reenacted the rescue effort annually on the fifth May of each year to pray and to commemorate the patriotic poet/courtier. In time, the practice of salvage boats evolved into dragon boat races, while the bamboo leaf wrapped dumpling—known as zongzi—became a ritual diet for that day. That was how the Fifth of May Festival became the world-renowned Dragon Boat Festival.

Today, a statue of Qu Yuan stands at his hometown of Ei-Zhang City, Hu Bei Province, China to commemorate the patriot poet.

Part IV

The Book of Lore

36

A LESSON IN ETTIQUETTE

The Chinese consider themselves a people of proper manners. It is that which distinguishes them from other living beings under the Heaven. It is through proper manners that people derive honor, and they strive above all things to attain proper behavior. Therefore to act with improper etiquette is to bring shame and dishonor to one's family, and more importantly, to one's ancestors.

Wang Mang Guan, better known as Old Master Wang, owned all the fertile farm fields around the small hamlet of Morh Fang. For his fifty-ninth birthday, Wang Huo Bao, his number one son, decided to invite the entire village to join in the birthday banquet. It was to be a major event, as Chinese celebrate birthdays in the years ending in the number nine. That's because the word "longevity" rhymes with that number, signifying a long-lasting life; whereas, the number ten sounds similar to the word for "death," not an auspicious way to celebrate one's birth.

The banquet invitation immediately became the hot topic of discussion in the village. Everyone was pleased with being invited to the festive occasion. However, it also posed a major dilemma; they wanted very much to attend the grand feast but were afraid of bringing shame to their ancestors by behaving improperly at the banquet. At the same time, they could not decline the invitation without giving offense to their landlord.

Chang San, the Village Chief, convened a general meeting to discuss the sensitive issue. He rose and coughed for attention. Mothers shushed their children into silence, as the village elder stroked his long flowing beard and raised his reedy voice "Honored brothers and sisters, we all know the purpose of this gathering. Old Master Wang has been a good landlord and his number one son has honored us with this invitation. I, for one, would like very much to attend the banquet, if for no other reason than to sample the fare of the rich." He paused pretentiously as the villagers politely chuckled at his ill attempt at wit. "If there is no other important issue to discuss, I would like to focus our attention on the subject of etiquette at the coming banquet."

A chorus of agreement followed his statement. "Now, does anyone have suggestions concerning proper behavior for this occasion?" A low murmur swept through the assembly, as each person conferred with family, friends, and neighbors.

Tsang Search, the village matchmaker, raised her hand and waved a bright red silk kerchief that had been tucked inside her shirtsleeve. The old Village Chief mentally grimaced and prepared for a dissertation from the long-tongued woman, who was renowned throughout the province for her loquacity. "Please enlighten us, Sister Tsang Serh?"

Tsang Serh rose and gently patted her perfectly styled coiffure, ensuring ample time for everyone to admire her over-rouged cheeks. She glanced about to make sure she had the attention of all present and then trilled, "What do the village elders think? I, like most of the people here, have neither education nor knowledge on such matters." She nodded her head and glowed at being the focus of everyone's attention. "Yes!" She nodded again for emphasis, "Yes! I think everyone would like to hear from the village elders first." Having properly announced her presence, she bowed in all directions then sat down to savor the villagers' admiration.

Her unusually short presentation caught everyone by surprise. After a lengthy silence, by ones and twos, the audience nodded and murmured their collective agreement.

The Village Chief shook his head apologetically; "I had already discussed the matter with the other elders. We thought of asking the District Magistrate for advice, but the water that is far away cannot put out the fire that rages at hand. We have not the time to dispatch someone to the district capital, and it is far from certain that the Magistrate would have an answer for us. He might even berate us for bothering him with such a trifling matter. Besides, it would announce our ignorance to the world. We must find a solution on our own."

Soon, the meeting began to lose focus and disintegrate into a social gathering. Then, suddenly, the butcher, Ah Nieu jumped up, knocking over his stool. The Village Chief seized the occasion to draw everyone's attention back to the issue at hand. "Ah Nieu, have you a suggestion? Please do enlighten us."

The much-embarrassed butcher swallowed and cleared his throat while scratching the back of his smooth, shiny pate. His sudden movement had been a reflexive reaction to a sharp and sudden mosquito bite. Saddled with the unsolicited attention, Ah Nieu felt compelled to give a face-saving response. He squinted his beady eyes, sucked in air through his teeth and grimaced, grasping for an innovative thought. Suddenly, his face beamed as he spied the shingled roof of the Buddhist temple.

He sniffed and rubbed his nose, then quickly dropped his hand as he restrained his own nervous habit. At length, he boomed out in his raspy voice, "I suggest we consult Master San Bao, Senior Monk of the Kuan Di Temple. Surely such a wise and learned person can direct us onto the right path."

A murmur of approval rippled through the audience. Many people seemed surprised at the sudden spark of brilliance in the normally dimwitted butcher.

A flicker of hope gleamed in Chang San's eyes, and he pounced on the solution. "Wonderful idea, however, instead of troubling Master San Bao, I propose we consult Ou-Yang Ben, who is not only a wise and learned scholar but also a son-in-law of Old Master Wang."

Next day, the village elders, led by Chang San, visited Ou-Yang Ben. Educated in Confucian philosophy and literature, he had only the year before won the title of 'Hsiu Tsai' - Superior Talent at the provincial level of the national examination. He was studying for the next year's national level examination at the Imperial Capital, which would be presided over by the Dragon Personage himself—the Imperial Emperor. The top three winners of the examination would be appointed to ministerial positions at the Imperial Court.

While Mrs. Ou-Yang served tea, the delegation noted Ou-Yang Ta-Bao sitting quietly on his father's lap. Chang San took note of the well-mannered boy and said, "Superior Talent Ou-Yang, you are to be congratulated for having such a polite and intelligent son. It must be the result of diligent tutoring by his well-educated parents."

"You are too kind. The boy is a difficult student, and often misbehaves," the scholar quickly countered in humility. However, the tender stroking hand and the doting eyes gave the lie to his words.

"As you know," Chang San continued, "the entire village has been invited to Wang Yuan Wai's birthday celebration. We are concerned about the proper form of behavior at the banquet, so as to avoid embarrassments to the host and ourselves, not to mention the possibility of insulting Wang Yuan Wai. We would like you to honor us by teaching us how to behave at your father-in-law's birthday banquet. The problem is that we cannot do our work and learn etiquette in the limited time available."

Ou-Yang Ben's face flushed with pride at having the Village Chief and the elders come to him for advice. The young scholar pursed his lips and waved his fan as he pondered their predicament. True to his training as an educated thinker, with a nod of his head, he offered up a simple solution. At the end of his proposal, the village elders were visibly impressed; education was definitely the key to success in life. As one, they rose and bowed their appreciation to the wise scholar.

On the evening of the appointed day, everyone, from the Village Chief to the beggar, gathered in front of Ou-Yang Ben's house, then walked en masse toward the great mansion at the eastern edge of the village.

Meanwhile, Old Rich Wang paced the marble floor. It was about time for the banquet to begin, but not one villager had yet arrived. For the tenth time, the Wang Huo Bao checked with the harried steward and confirmed that written invitations had indeed been sent, accompanied by a crier to announce the event for the benefit of the illiterates. There was no error regarding the date and time of the banquet. Finally, everyone breathed a sigh of relief when an excited and jubilant servant ran in to report the approach of a large mass of populace. Old Rich Wang hitched up the front of his robe and hurried to greet his guests at the main entrance.

The Village Chief, accompanied by Ou-Yang Ben and the other village elders, walked in the fore, followed by the men folk bearing traditional birthday gifts of potted bamboo plants and a long silk robe. Women and children walked at the rear of the crowd. Bamboo leaves remain green throughout the year, symbolizing their wishing an everlasting youth to the host. The robe was made from silk spun and woven jointly by the village women and intricately embroidered with one hundred "long life" characters.

Wearing a broad smile, Old Rich Wang stepped forward to greet the guests. He paused in surprise at the sight of his number ten son-in-law at the fore of the villagers. Ou-Yang Ben halted three paces in front of his father-in-law, and bowed from the waist while singing his salutation for the festive occasion—"MAY YOU OUTLIVE THE SOUTHERN MOUNTAINS, FATHER-IN-LAW." Before the host could respond, the entire village populace bowed and bellowed—"MAY YOU OUTLIVE THE SOUTHERN MOUNTAINS, FATHER-IN-LAW." Old Rich Wang was bewildered and confused, but nevertheless, graciously welcomed them into the mansion.

Flabbergasted, and embarrassed at the dumb villagers for greeting Wang Yuan Wai as their father-in-law, Ou-Yang Ben resolved to keep a stern face and not speak to anyone unless spoken to, so as to avoid further awkward humiliation. As previously instructed, the villagers aped his every gesture. Ou-Yang Ben's taciturn behavior resulted in a house full of severely reticent guests that looked more like creditors than well wishers. The few attempts at small talk from Wang and his family met with friendly words grunted through tightly pursed lips.

The young scholar sat silently and fumed at the stupidity of the country bumpkins. Suddenly, he felt a tug at his sleeve. A sideward glance took in Ta-Bao, seeking his father's attention. The forbidding visage softened, as the father bent over to listen to his son. "Father, I need to go pee-pee," said the boy.

"Ta Bao, it is impolite to say pee-pee in public, you should remember that."

"Well, what should I say then?"

Ou-Yang Ben pondered before responding, "You should say, 'I want to sing.' It sounds much more polite and proper."

"Father, I want to sing."

"Now, that's a good, smart boy. Let's go, I'll take you." Their departure immediately created a queue waiting for turns at the honey chamber, and the single bucket quickly overflowed.

At a loss as to the cause of the odd behaviors of his guests, Wang Huo Bao decided to hurry the agenda of the evening. Perhaps food would brighten the demeanor of this laconic gathering. He ordered servants to begin the feast as he ushered the villagers into the great hall, where a battalion of servants in new silk robes waited on sixty tables; one table for every year of Wang Yuan Wai's age, plus one to make it an even number of tables.

Ou-Yang Ben tried to act nonchalant; however, his attempt at composure quickly fell apart when he realized that every villager would wait for him to sample a particular dish, then follow suit. As a result, some dishes were consumed quickly, while others were left untouched.

In resignation, Ou-Yang Ben decided to concentrate on enjoying the meal. He helped himself to a large portion of the giant steamed carp. Suddenly, his eyes bulged in consternation, as a fish bone got lodged in his throat. He gagged and attempted to remove the fish bone with his fingers. Finally, with a loud hawk, he managed to cough out the offending barb. Peering through watery eyes, his worst fear was confirmed. Many of his diligent pupils were still standing with their fingers in their mouths.

Trembling with rage and despair, Ou-Yang Ben tried to regain his dignity with a sip of the shark fin soup; however, his quivering hand failed him and the porcelain spoon slid through slippery saliva coated fingers to smash against the floor. The crashing sound had barely subsided when a crescendo of breaking china followed suit. Crying tears of shame and frustration, Ou-Yang Ben dashed out of the mansion, leaving his wife to deal with the discourtesy to her father. His departure set off an exodus of villagers, leaving the stunned and baffled host to celebrate his birthday without a single guest.

On their way home, the villagers shook their heads in collective bewilderment. All agreed that while the food was delicious, the strange etiquette of the rich people was, to say the least, beyond comprehension.

That evening, Ou-Yang Ben stoically received the village elders, as they profusely voiced the admiration and gratitude of the entire village. He thought it wise not to explain the villagers' faux pas; it would only cause further embarrassment for all parties concerned.

Closing the door behind his grateful guests, Ou-Yang Ben dragged his tired body into the bedchamber. In the flickering candlelight, he saw the rough outline of Ta-Bao snuggled against his mother. The sight of the boy brought up the memory of the entire village lined up to visit the honey chamber, invoking an irresistible chuckle. His foul mood dissipated as Ou-Yang Ben thought of the mob of villagers tramping through each other's wastewater. A smile widened his face as he crawled into bed next to his son.

In the middle of the night, Ou-Yang Ben felt a small pair of groping hands tugging at his robe, and a persistent voice demanding his attention. "Pa pa, pa pa."

"What is it, little precious?" He reflexively mumbled a response at the familiar voice.

"I want to sing."

"What did you say?"

"I want to sing."

Ou-Yang Ben strained his cobwebby eyes, but in the darkness, he could not even see his own fingers. He murmured sleepily, "Do you know what time it is? Everybody is sleeping. It is not the proper time for singing."

But the boy would not be denied. He whimpered, "But, I want to sing, and I need to sing."

"All right, all right, you can sing. Now, don't wake up your mother. Sing very softly into my ear."

37
THE DAO OF TEA

Since ancient time, the Chinese have consumed tea as a part of their daily life. Initially, people drank tea as herbal medicine to improve their health. It had since become the most popular beverage around the globe. No self-respecting Chinese family would be found without tea in its cupboard.

Head hung low, Joe plodded dejectedly down the sidewalk. Martha's scathing words still burning his ears— "Don't come back until you have gotten some lead in your pencil!" *Viagra required a physician's prescription and was not cheap; besides, does it work on premature ejaculation?* Humiliated and angry, Joe was at the end of his wits; he was resigned to spend the night on the sofa hugging Nicky, the French poodle.

A movement at the periphery of his vision drew his attention. Joe lifted his head and spotted Mr. Wong trimming a hedge. A ray of hope sparkled in Joe's eyes. *Those slant eyes were well known for their refined sexual expertise; perhaps he had a solution for my short-coming. Normally I wouldn't have the time of day for him, but desperate times called for desperate measures.* "Mr. Wong, good morning," Joe waved his hand as he crossed the well-manicured lawn to approach the swarthy Chinese, "nice day isn't it?"

Wong noticed the approaching burly *guai-lao* (foreign devil) and nodded dubiously in salutation. "Good morning Mr. Joe; what can I do for you?"

Joe hesitated then decided to forge ahead, "You are a man of sophistication and experience. I would like to know if you are knowledgeable regarding the erotic arts." Wong was not sure what Joe was getting at but did not want to lose face by appearing ignorant. The Chinese nodded a shallow toothy grin and waited for Joe to continue the conversation. Undaunted by the taciturn response, Joe persisted, "I want to know how your people do it? In bed I mean, how do you satisfy your partners?"

Finally, Wong seemed to have perceived the purpose of the neighborly surprise visit. "Well, why don't you come inside the house and we'll discuss the matter." Wong ushered Joe into a seat then brought out a tray with a pot of tea with two cups. He poured and served the tea then took a seat opposite from his guest. "Now, what exactly is it that you wish to know?"

"It's like this," Joe hemmed and hawed as he disclosed his difficulty. Wong thought for a moment then pointed a finger at the tea, "the answer is very simple, it lies in the tea in front of you."

"What tea is this? How much do I need to drink? And where do I buy it?"

The host again presented his toothy smile and waved his hands in the negative, "the secret is not the tea, but how you consume it." He nodded his head sagely then continued, "What you must do is prepare a tall glass of tea before you mount the meat cushion."

"Meat cushion?"

"Yes, that's how you practice 'the Zen of Happiness'—on a meat cushion, your sex partner."

Joe grinned and nodded. "And how exactly do you use the tea to prolong the Zen of Happiness?"

"Once you are in position you count your strokes, silently to yourself of course. This way it diverts part of your mind away from your sexual act, to reduce the effect of the stimulation. When you reached the count of ten, stop your amorous activity and take a sip of the tea. The pause provides time for your body to cool off from the excitement before you return to the arena. This technique will prolong your duration in the battle of the mattress until she climaxes, and then you may proceed to complete the task to your satisfaction."

That night, Martha walked into the bedroom to find dim lighting, soft music, and her naked husband in bed with the cover turned down. The faint fragrance of jasmine floated in the air; however, she did not notice its source—a tall glass of tea that stood in a dark corner of the nightstand.

Martha slowly disrobed, noticing Joe following her every move with a sly grin. For some reason, she thought his eyebrows looked a bit slanted. As she climbed into bed, Martha reached over to turn out the light, but Joe intercepted her hand. "I want to see you when we do it; your passion inflamed face excites me." It would be a disaster should he knock over the tea by accident in the midst of their amorous encounter.

He rolled over to lie next to Martha and started his ritual foreplay. Before long, Joe inserted his engorged member into her and commenced thrusting. She was pleasantly surprised by Joe's sudden aggressiveness and was more than willing to see how far he was going with this new found vitality. However, Martha quickly noticed Joe's movements were slower, almost mechanical. He appeared to be distracted but otherwise functional.

'1, 2, 3, 4, 5, 6, 7, 8, 9, 10' Joe stopped his stroking, "excuse me, I am thirsty." He reached over and took a pull of the tea then resumed rutting. '1, 2, 3, 4, 5, 6, 7, 8, 9, 10' Joe stopped again, "I need a drink." He sipped another mouthful and went back to his lover's chore. Joe felt invigorated. Wong's trick was working; by concentrating on the stroke count, Joe did manage to dampen the mental and physical effects of the sexual stimulation. He had lasted longer than he ever did before and was still going strong. The periodic tea breaks further extended his physical stamina with Martha. Things could not be better he thought, as he paused again and reached for another mouthful of the Jasmine tea. Just as he set down the glass, a smashing blow to the side of his head sent him tumbling onto the floor. Stunned, Joe shook the stars out of his head; finally, he found his voice, "Why...what...what was that for?"

Through teary eyes, he saw Martha towering over him at the edge of the bed, fuming with anger. "Where in the hell did you learn to screw like a Chinaman? ...Oops."

38
THE IMPERIAL CHAMPION

Emperor Qian Long relished the icy tension at the Imperial Court. The verbal jousts between the great lords and ministers were like a chess match, with pieces hidden from view. To him, keeping track of the shifting alliances of rival political factions was a game of mental gymnastics, it kept the mind sharp.

This time the subject of the squabble was both joyous and odious. Joyful because the imperial ruler would soon be celebrating his fiftieth birthday, but odious for the reminder that time spared no one—not even for the most powerful man under Heaven. He listened with half an ear as the courtiers argued for control of the agenda at the coming gala, but the other part of the imperial mind strayed. The Son of Heaven thought about his most recent jaunt through the rivers and lakes of his realm; traveling incognito, he'd even gotten a workout with his fighting skills in actual combat. Truth-be-known he'd almost died at the hands of some unknown ruffians, if not for the timely intervention of a yet unidentified savior. Nevertheless, it was an exhilarating experience. He'd never felt as alive as he had on the brink of death.

He'd traveled incognito with a single bodyguard, Jing Curd, the Commander of the Imperial Guards. While taking in the sights of the scenic West Lake, they'd seen a group of local toughs mistreating a beggar. The emperor's sense of justice made him intervene. The captain drew his sword but was overwhelmed and out numbered. The gang then turned on the emperor. The imperial ruler knocked down a couple of toughs with his staff but was about to go the way of the captain when a young warrior appeared; his big knife flashed with gallant speed and scattered the bullies like an autumn wind through fallen leaves.

Qian Long rushed to tend to the injured captain, and never got a chance to properly thank the warrior for his help. His savior had disappeared after he had beaten off the bullies. Oh, how the emperor wished to be back trekking through the realm again; to meet the people, sample their fare and find that young warrior.

Inevitably, the emperor was summoned back to reality. The portly First Minister of the Right bowed then waddled forward, "Your Imperial Majesty, I propose a national poetry contest to commemorate your nativity. The theme shall center on the great accomplishments of your enlightened reign and your eternal existence."

The emperor prided himself as an accomplished scholar and often dabbled in poetry and calligraphy. Minister Gi, a renowned poet, thought the occasion as another opportunity to show off his literary expertise and gain more honor from his master. Qian Long felt the demands of time on his aging body. He did not want to hear poetry lauding his past glories and be reminded of the inevitable end. The old monarch shook his head and frowned with disinterest, and the dejected minister bowed and backed away to his position at the fore of the ranks of courtiers that stood on the right side of the great hall.

The First Minister of the Left, the tall bowlegged Mongolian General Wokuotai, stepped forward, "Ole Master who lives ten thousand years, may I humbly suggest a cross-country horse race to celebrate the imperial birthday? The race shall start from the westernmost city in Qinghai province and end on the parade ground of the Forbidden City." Everyone knew the emperor liked fast steeds. If accepted, the event would undoubtedly raise the status of Mongolian horsemen in the empire—who under the Heaven but a Mongol could have the skill and the stamina to win such a race? The emperor stroked his beard as he pondered the idea, but he shook his head and waved the Mongolian general back to his position. A lull lingered while courtiers digested the negative reception suffered by the two senior ministers.

Ho Sheng, Chief Eunuch of the Imperial Realm, stepped out from behind the emperor and lifted his staff of office. In addition to being the Administrator of the Imperial Palace, he also was the emperor's confidant; in fact, he'd been the Imperial Personage's childhood playmate. Although the Chief Eunuch ranked far below the lords and ministers, he had the emperor's ear, and therefore political power. Those that underestimated the unassuming eunuch paid for the error dearly. Now Ho Sheng spied another chance to spit in the eyes of those aristocratic snobs. He recalled his master's passion for the martial arts, that tidbit of knowledge just became invaluable.

"Ole Master that lives ten thousand years, this worthless servant would like to suggest a martial arts contest, an Imperial Tournament. The winner shall receive prizes in gold, plus the title of 'Imperial Champion of the Realm.' In addition, since the position of the Commander of the Imperial Guards is still vacant, that could be the reward as well. Who is more suited to be in charge of the safety of your honored Dragon Personage, than the Imperial Champion of the Realm?"

The verbal jousting among the courtiers had begun to bore Qian Long. Ho Sheng's petition came like a breath of fresh air. The emperor roused himself out of his daydreaming and shook cobwebs from his mind. Interest glinted in those golden imperial eyes as he shifted to a more comfortable position on the dragon throne. The chief eunuch's suggestion was unique and definitely more interesting than the traditional fare of operas, poetry contests, circuses and horse races.

"Once again old friend, you have come through with a gem. We consider that an excellent idea. To make it more interesting, the tournament shall be open to all peoples, regardless of their nationality or station in society. A general amnesty shall be in effect for the duration of the tournament, so that everyone may join in the competition. It shall be a true championship contest under the Heaven." Aware that his childhood playmate was also a master of Tai Qi boxing, the emperor added, "And you Ho Sheng, since it was your idea, are hereby appointed as the Tournament Director, responsible for its organization and conduct."

The lords and ministers sputtered and fumed in frustration. The First Minister of the Right protested, "Master, to have armed common riffraff and foreign devils parading freely inside the Forbidden City is beyond comprehension. I am concerned with the peace and tranquility of your Imperial Personage. Lastly, you wished everyone under the Heaven be allowed to participate. Should a foreign barbarian win the contest, your personal safety will be in the hands of a foreign devil."

Qian Long was not in the habit of changing his mind, he snorted aloud at the preposterous nature of the petition. The minister quivered at the imperial displeasure then bowed his head in obedience and retreated to his post. The other courtiers knew the emperor's stubborn streak, and

The first minister's experience was not one to be repeated. They muted their dissent and resigned to wishing for a disastrous outcome at the contest, so as to embarrass the chief eunuch for his outrageous idea.

Ho Sheng kowtowed to the emperor and stepped forward to accept the appointment edict then swaggered out of the court under the scathing glares of his colleagues.

The next day, battalions of imperial messengers rode out of Beijing, the seat of the imperial realm, to post proclamations throughout the land:

> *By Imperial decree, there shall be a martial arts contest to celebrate the emperor's birthday. The winner shall receive ten thousand taels of gold, two concubines, and the title of Champion of the Realm, along with an appointment as Commander of the Imperial Guards.*
>
> *Preliminary contests shall commence three days prior to the emperor's birthday. The final competition shall take place in the imperial garden of the Forbidden City, on the final day of the imperial birthday celebrations, as the final program of the Imperial Festivities.*

Messengers delivered a copy of the imperial edict to each of the diplomatic missions in the Capital, extending the imperial invitation to all foreign devils under the Heaven.

Wang Wu had been a student of Dong-Fang Chang Sheng, the Dragon Head Big Brother of the Beggar Society, and a martial arts champion. The Society counted all beggars of the realm as its members. It acted as a guild to regulate and protect its membership against people that prey on the weaker caste of the society. For his unique skill with the blade, the young warrior acquired the nickname of 'Big Knife Wang Wu.'

The proclamation about the imperial tournament perked Wang Wu's interest. It would be an opportunity to match his fighting skills against the top fighters of the realm, perhaps the world. If nothing else, it would be a chance to tour Beijing at the old man emperor's expense.

Wang Wu registered for the tournament at the local provincial governor's office. The magistrate recognized Wang Wu and knew of his ability with the blade. The official handed a letter to Wang Wu, "This is your certificate of eligibility for the contest, and the authority to commandeer transportation and meal facilities for traveling to Beijing. Good luck, bring back honors for our city."

At the imperial capital, the letter secured courteous treatment from the tournament staff. Ten days afterward, he entered the preliminary competitions. Wang Wu fought the bolo of a South American gaucho, followed by a Shaolin warrior monk's staff, a Tibetan monk's head-snatcher, then three other warriors of the realm. He thought the head-snatcher was a most unique weapon. It was a flat cloth pouch with a ring of sharp blades inside. The Tibetan monk—also known as a lama—threw the weapon like a disc at his enemy and controlled its flight with a long thin chain. The trick was to throw it over a person's head then pull on it to trap and sever the head of the victim. It was a silent and deadly assassin's tool, but ineffective against an alert opponent.

During the contest against the lama, Wang Wu charged straight at the opponent, negating the foe's reach advantage and complicated the control of the head-snatcher. A quick slap of the big knife against the lama's wrist made the man drop his weapon and ended that fight. By the end of the third day of the contest, Wang Wu emerged as a finalist at the imperial tournament.

On the morning of the emperor's birthday, five contestants followed a blue silk-robed eunuch into the imperial garden inside the Forbidden City. As they stood in a row awaiting the arrival of the emperor, the warriors measured each other. Only then did Wang Wu realize that the rumors he had heard were true, he was the only Chinese to have survived the elimination rounds.

One other oriental made it to the finals. He went by the name of Miyamoto Muzashi, an infamous pirate captain from the Land of the Rising Sun. His pirates raided the eastern coasts of China. Wang Wu had never met the pirate but knew the man by reputation as a skilled fighter with the two-handed longsword, known as the katana. A ceremonial short sword accompanied the long blade at the man's waist. Supposedly, the short sword was used in ritual suicide in the event of defeat in combat. Rumor had it that Miyamoto Muzashi could leap into the air and decapitate a bird in flight. Whatever Muzashi's character flaw may have been, Wang Wu admired the man for the nerve to enter the imperial capital with a price on his head. The pirate wore a blue robe decorated with large white chrysanthemum floral designs.

Next to Muzashi stood a tall foreign devil with long curly dark brown hair that cascaded under a broad-brimmed purple hat, topped with a plume of purple ostrich feather. He wore a strange but rich looking royal purple cape that had rectangular front and back pieces of equal size; a large golden cross emblazoned the middle of each rectangle. Silver lilies trimmed with gold thread decorated each corner of the cape. The man sported a thin but well-manicured mustache that turned sharply upward at the ends. At his waist, hung from a broad cross-shoulder strap, was a long thin sword, an epee, which Wang Wu had heard of but never seen. The escorting eunuch introduced the tall western barbarian as Da Tang Yang, from the western kingdom of Flance and purported to be a royal guardsman for the king of that nation.

The third foreigner seemed too short and puny to be a martial arts practitioner. In spite of the heat of the summer day, the man was covered from head to toe in not only leather but black leather. He wore a broad black-brimmed felt hat with a high crown, a black leather vest, and black leather coveralls over black pants plus a pair of pointy-toed black leather boots. The only not black item was the ring of silver coins that encircled the crown of his hat. For a weapon, he carried a short black thunder stick, which of course, hung on his left hip from a black leather holster on a black leather belt. Wang Wu warned himself to be extra careful with the little man, for he had seen the effectiveness of gunpowder weapons in proper hands. The man called himself Bill Li and claimed to be a cow herder from the land of the Golden Mountain. Wang Wu thought Golden Mountain must be a truly rich and barbaric land; if a mere cow herder could acquire a thunder stick for self-protection, and be proficient with it.

The last foreigner was dressed in a garish green outfit, complete with a triangular green cap that sat atilt on his head, decorated with a long green pheasant feather. Wang Wu chuckled at the sight; no Chinese would be caught dead with a green hat. To the Chinese, 'a person that wore a green hat' was one who had been cuckolded. However, despite his laughable outfit, the tall man appeared lean, fit, well-armed and knowledgeable in the use of the tools of his trade. He sported a long broadsword to the left of his waist, a dagger on his right hip, a full quiver of arrows on his back and a long, fancy green bow in his left hand. He proclaimed himself the prince of a forest in an island kingdom named Ingrand and wished to be addressed as Lo Bin Han.

As for himself, Wang Wu wore a simple short-red warrior's tunic. A length of bright red silk that tied his long tonsured queue atop his head. At his left hip, in a sharkskin scabbard, hung a long curved knife that broadened near the top then sharpened to a needle point.

A young eunuch walked up holding a silk pouch on a lacquered tray; he sang out to the contestants in a high-pitched soprano, "Masters, please take one disk from the pouch. It will designate your order of appearance in the tournament." Three young courtiers in scholarly robes quickly translated the announcement to the foreigners. The young eunuch walked up and presented his tray, each finalist reached into the drawstring sack and withdrew a gold-trimmed white jade disk. On the disk, carved with blue, red and green inlays were finely detailed dragons. Wang Wu examined his disc and saw five small grimacing dragons on its polished surface, designating him as the last in the order of appearance.

A series of crashing gongs and bleating trumpets at the entrance to the imperial garden announced the arrival of the emperor and his entourage. A long line of musicians led the procession then came a company of imperial guards, a twenty-four-man palanquin floated amidst the second company of guardsmen, and the third company of guards trailed behind. A mixed group of eunuchs and senior court functionaries followed behind them. In the rear, a final group of junior officials, foreign dignitaries, and local municipal elites shuffled in a mob into the garden.

The palanquin settled down on the stone paved path in front of a large red pavilion with a blue tiled roof. The emperor emerged from the palanquin, brushed away the hands of two eunuchs who attempted to assist in his disembarkation from the ornate man powered carriage. He strode in long majestic strides to the throne inside the pavilion, trailed by a dozen servants, each carried assorted items that the emperor might need or desire. Once the Dragon Personage had been seated, a detachment of the guardsmen marched to their protective positions in and around the pavilion. Then the throng of lords, ministers, princes, dukes, foreign dignitaries and local elites jostled for positions to be near the emperor and have a good view of the contest. Meanwhile, the remaining guardsmen formed a three rank deep blocking force between the emperor and the tournament field.

Qian Long nodded at Ho Sheng, who bowed then waved his staff at a junior eunuch. The young eunuch waved his staff and the musicians crashed out a string of quick and rhythmic notes from their gongs and drums. Ho Sheng took haughty steps to the fore as the crowd fell silent; he bowed to the emperor then waved the five finalists forward. Prior to entering the pavilion, each contestant left his weapons with the guards.

Ho Sheng self-importantly sniffed and rubbed his nose then strutted to the entrance of the pavilion and turned to face the audience. He took a deep breath and sang out, "Master that lives ten thousand years, members of the imperial court and honored guests. I am Ho Sheng, Chief Eunuch of the Realm and by imperial appointment, the director of this tournament and the judge of this final competition." He paused for effect and gloated at his fellow courtiers before he continued, "We have here, in front of you, five finalists for the martial arts championship contest. I will introduce them in the order of their coming performance. Da Tang Yang, the royal guardsman from the kingdom of Flance; Lo Bin Han, a prince from the island kingdom of Ingrand; Bill Li, from the land of the Golden Mountain; Miyamoto Muzashi from the Land of the Rising Sun; and our own Wang Wu the Big Knife of the West Lake.

"As this is the day we celebrate the emperor's birthday, there shall be no death or bloodshed to mar the harmony of the occasion. Any violator will be disqualified. Thus, we will not have the one-on-one match between the contestants. Instead, we require that each person gives a demonstration of his martial skill. Since the winner shall also become the Commander of the Imperial Guards, we shall be judging for the skill and the intellect of each warrior. The contestants have drawn lots to determine the order of their appearance. Each man shall devise his own method of demonstrating his fighting skill. The ingenuity in design and the skill of the actual presentation shall bear equal weight in deciding the winner of the competition. "

The emperor was surprised and dismayed that only one person of his realm had made it into the final round of the contest, bringing to mind the earlier warning from The First Minister. The presence of the much feared and hated eastern ocean pirate captain only made the matters worse. The frown of his imperial brow sent beads of sweat down the spine of the chief eunuch. However, the frown dissipated as the emperor's eyes landed on the Chinese warrior. He smiled then nodded and waved his hand to signal the beginning of the contest.

Ho Sheng bowed again to the emperor then headed for the grassy area in front of the pavilion which served as the competition ground.

The contestants backed out of the pavilion to retrieve their arms then headed toward Ho Sheng and the tournament field. Da Tang Yang stepped out of the group, doffed his hat and swept it over the ground as he bowed to the emperor and the tournament director. "Sire, to assist in my presentation, may I request the presence of one of your imperial guardsman?" Ho Sheng nodded his head and dispatched a young eunuch to summon an off-duty guardsman.

Within one incense's burning time, a soldier in full dress regalia appeared at the bend of the garden path and marched toward the emperor in the pavilion. As he walked past Da Tang Yang, the epee danced forth from the Flanchman's side. The guardsman felt a stream of cold air about his body, accompanied by images of a thousand flashing sword points thrusting at him from every direction. Instinctively he reached for his broadsword, but it was no longer there. He felt a lightening of weight followed by a crashing sound. Before he had recovered from the sudden attack the vision of sword blades had disappeared. Other pieces of his garments and equipage followed the broadsword in floating or falling off of his body.

The crowd roared in astonishment and cheered, as the guardsman stood uncovered from the neck down to his knees. Only his helmet and boots remained on his person, and there was not a whit of a scratch on the hairy dark brown skin.

The soldier stared with horror at his emperor, who was laughing along with members of the audience. The guardsman realized he was no longer presentable to the emperor and decided to retreat before he was condemned for being out of uniform or exposing himself to the Son of Heaven. The soldier removed his helmet with his right hand and used it to cover his private parts as he bowed to the emperor then turned to escape from the garden.

Da Tang Yang sheathed the epee then doffed his hat to the emperor and the audience to signify the end of his presentation. As he retreated from the field amid thunderous roars of approval, Lo Bin Han stepped forward. He bowed to the emperor then, without waiting for an acknowledgment, turned and in one smooth motion, let fly three arrows at the retreating guardsman. The first two missiles peeled off the soles of the man's boots and pinned them to the ground. As the soldier tripped and fell, the third missile zipped in between his legs and knocked away his makeshift codpiece. While the unwilling live target tumbled and rolled, two more shafts succeeded in stripping the last tattered bits of boots from his feet, leaving him naked as the moment of his birth.

Once again, the crowd cheered and clapped at the virtuoso performance. Lo Bin Han removed his conical cap and bowed to the emperor, before exiting the arena.

Bill Li rose from his seat, hitched up his gun belt and walked bow-legged to the front of the pavilion. He tipped his hat at the emperor and drawled, "Howdy, your majesty. Them boys done did a fine job with them toothpick and whatnot. I'm gonna have a rough time topping their do-thats." Just then, an angry scream cut through the air, and a tall naked man charged out of the bushes toward the tournament field. A squad of guardsmen moved to interdict the intruder. They quickly recognized the man as their erstwhile comrade, who had only recently been publicly disarmed and disrobed. People saw the soldiers swing their spears into the air then joined their naked comrade in fleeing toward the pavilion.

It appeared that the naked man had sought refuge in the bushes, but a hive of hornets contested their home turf. Under the attack of the stinging insects, the man had inadvertently run in the direction of the imperial pavilion.

The dark-buzzing cloud of hornets panicked the crowd, some tried to escape but were blocked by the lines of guardsmen intent on protecting their emperor. Amidst the turmoil, a series of rolling thunderclaps crashed into everyone's eardrums. In the ensuing silence, people forgot about the hornets, which had returned to their nest; everyone looked in the direction of the noise then focused on Bill Li, who casually raised his weapon and blew smoke from its barrel. He reloaded the gun before returning it to the holster then walked up to Ho Sheng. Bill Li reached up with his leather-gloved hand and from the top of the eunuch's round gauze cap, picked off six hornets. The insects were in perfect condition but knocked unconscious by the shock wave generated by the close transit of bullets near their bodies.

Ho Sheng explained Bill Li's accomplishment to the audience then one by one the hornets awakened and crawled about Bill Li's hand before launching themselves into the air. The audience once again clapped and oohed-and-aahed with excitement.

While people tried to recover from the chaotic chain of events, Miyamoto Muzashi walked into the center of the clearing. He grunted a salute toward the emperor then leaped forward with a roaring battle cry. The long sword jumped into the pirate's hands, with which he continuously slashed the air. Soon, an amazed roar erupted from the crowd, as they saw, wrapped in a cage of flashing sword blades was, a single live hornet. Miyamoto Muzashi maintained the entrapment for a ten count then gave another shout and the sword disappeared into its scabbard.

The pirate captain bowed to the thundering applause from the audience, while Wang Wu walked up and bowed to the emperor.

By then, every member of the Imperial Court, from the emperor to the lowest ranking eunuch had a nagging thought. *Would Wang Wu be able to uphold the honor of the realm, in the face of such stiff competition? If Wang Wu should fail to measure up, Ho Sheng would have the additional problem of deciding the winner from the first four contestants; whoever Ho Sheng chose as the winner, it would surely invoke a round of diplomatic protests from the embassies of the losing nations.* Privately, the imperial lords and ministers silently prayed for Wang Wu to fail. The embarrassment of the face-losing incident would ruin Ho Sheng, the man responsible for the insane spectacle. A foreign devil in command of the Imperial Guards would become a shameful reminder of Ho Sheng's folly. Not to mention the insanity of having a skilled barbarian warrior stand close watch over the safety of the Dragon Personage.

Well acquainted with the thought process of his colleagues, beads of cold sweat gathered on Ho Sheng's brow, and his scarred private parts shriveled further into his body. He silently prayed, *oh, Amidah Buddha, I vow to make a pilgrimage to the White Horse Temple and build you a new thirteen-tiered pagoda, if only Wang Wu will get me out of this delicate predicament.*

The audience grew silent as Wang Wu nonchalantly turned then quickly crouched, his right hand darted toward the left side of his body. A few people with keen eyes saw an arc of light flash through the air before Wang Wu turned to bow again to the emperor, signaling the completion of his performance. A rustling murmur undulated through the audience, as everyone inquired about details of Wang Wu's demonstration. Finally, Ho Sheng approached Wang Wu. "Warrior Wang, please excuse these failing eyes of a dawdling old man, but what exactly did you do?"

Wang Wu pointed at the ground by his right boot. "Sir, that is the subject of my demonstration."

Ho Sheng looked down and saw a hornet buzzing and spinning madly in circles on the ground. Wang Wu bent down and with a quick sweep of his right hand caught the hornet by the wings. It struggled futilely with its wings pinned back between Wang Wu's fingers. The judge barked, and a young eunuch ran up with a glass jar to catch the hornet. Ho Sheng raised the jar to eye level and adjusted his bifocals, but could not detect anything special that had been done to the hornet. "Contestant Wang, please explain the details of your performance."

"Sire, may I respectfully request the services of the imperial physician."

The Chief Eunuch nodded and waved a hand toward a young eunuch, who ran to the audience and returned with a bespectacled old man in tow, trailed by two of his own assistants.

Wang Wu bowed to the elderly physician. "Sire, please examine this hornet under the microscope and advise the judge of your findings." The old man nodded with self-importance then pointed to the older member of his assistants. The young man sped off then returned a short while later with three servants. Two of them shuffled forward with a table, while the third carried a small black box. He set the box on the table and retrieved a microscope from inside the box.

Under the direction of the imperial physician, the assistants managed to position the hornet under the microscope. The old doctor peered into the lens and adjusted the magnification knobs. He looked and looked again, then took a third look before raising his head to lift his spectacles and stare with wrinkled brow at Wang Wu in amazement. The old physician trundled with a wry grin to the judge and whispered into his ear. The Chief Eunuch shot an astonished glance in Wang Wu's direction, then walked over for a personal look into the lens of the microscope. When he rose from the apparatus, a wide smile decorated the corners of his mouth as he entered the pavilion to confer with the emperor.

By this time, the buzzing among the audience had risen to a crescendo. At a nod of agreement from his master, the Chief Eunuch strutted to the center of the clearing and clapped his hands for silence, and a round of crashing gongs reinforced that order. When silence reigned, Ho Sheng announced in his loud soprano. "Your Imperial Majesty, honored dignitaries and guests, I have the pleasure of presenting to you, Wang Wu, the Martial Arts Champion of the Realm." A chorus of cheers, intermixed with not a few jeers of disagreement and disgruntlement rumbled through the audience. Ho Sheng broke off his announcement and waved for silence before continuing, "And the new Commander of the Imperial Guards." Ho Sheng had to wave a third time for the audience to quiet down before he screeched out the result of the imperial physician's findings. The deafening silence from the crowd signified muted accord with his judgment in awarding the prize to Wang Wu.

Ho Sheng summoned a squad of Imperial Guardsmen to protect the microscope, as members of the Imperial Court, led by the emperor, approached the table to congratulate the Champion, and examine the hornet—the newest eunuch of the Forbidden City.

That evening the emperor summoned his new Commander of the Imperial Guards. "Commander Wang, were you at the West Lake around spring of last year?"

"Yes, Your Majesty."

"Do you recall chasing off a group of ruffians who were bullying a beggar and two visitors to that city?"

39
THE IMPRERIAL EMBASSADOR

Li Hong Zhang, Marquis Suyi of the First Class and Viceroy of Zhili, was arguably the most famous Imperial Chinese envoy to visit the United States. A pompous but wily official of the Imperial Court, he left an unusual legacy in the United States of America.

In 1896, the Imperial Ching Empire dispatched Viceroy Li Hong Zhang as Ambassador-At-Large on a fact-finding tour of the world. On arrival at San Francisco, the mayor gave a long and windy welcoming speech then presented the key to the city along with a purebred pedigreed poodle to the imperial envoy. The next day, the viceroy attended a Texas style BBQ, followed by an evening as the guest of honor at the San Francisco Symphony.

After the mayor settled himself in the balcony box seat, he exchanged salutations with his guest then asked, "Viceroy Li, how do you like the dog I gave you. It was the pick of the litter from my champion poodle."

The Marquis nodded agreeably, "Very good, very good, it tasted very good."

Flabbergasted, for once the garrulous Mayor remained strangely silent for the remainder of the evening.

At the end of the show, reporters besieged the viceroy with questions on a wide range of issues. At length, the lifestyle reporter for the San Francisco Chronicle inquired, "Viceroy Li, which part of the evening's musical presentation do you favor?"

"The beginning part," came the quick reply.

"Do you mean Camille Saint-Saens's Number 3 in C minor?"

"No, before that."

"Tchaikovsky's Number 6 in B minor? Beethoven's Number 3 in E flat?" The imperial envoy gave negative head shakes to each of the man's query. At length, it dawned on the reporter that the viceroy had been referring to the beginning of the symphony presentation when the orchestra was tuning their instruments.

At the end of the evening, with a mutual sigh of relief, the viceroy and his host bid farewell then mounted their respective coaches to return to their residences. Along the way, Li's stomach growled at him. The ambassador remembered that he barely ate at the BBQ. *No self-respecting Chinese would eat bloody red meat and feed corn that was fit only for animals. These western foreign devils have truly barbarian dining habits.* He shouted to his aide, over the noise of the rumbling carriage, "Go to Chinatown and find me a Chinese restaurant!"

The aide decided against reminding the ambassador of the lateness of the hour. It would not have made any difference anyway. As the representative of the emperor, the viceroy would not and could not be refused. The carriage stopped at a small Chinese restaurant. When the aide jumped out of the carriage, he realized that a trio of reporters had been tailing the Chinese envoy for newsworthy tidbits.

San Mao had been dreaming of attending a banquet with the elders of the Chinese Benevolent Association. Suddenly one the waiters dropped a large bowl of soup, and the loud crash awakened the restaurateur from his slumber. Continued loud banging at his front door chased the cobwebs out of his mind. "Who is it?" He shouted at the ignorant who intruded on his dream.

"Open up, in the name of the emperor!" came the commanding response.

"Alright, I'm coming, I'm coming." He ran to open the door without bothering to pull on a shirt. The sight of the Imperial Viceroy sent San Mao to his knees and banged his forehead on the dirty floor. "Master," he uttered then waited to be spoken to.

The blue robed aide stepped forward, "Rise. The viceroy is hungry, go cook something hot for the master." He took a look at the reporters and added, "Make enough food for five people. Be quick about it, don't make the master wait too long."

San Mao banged his head on the ground one more time then rose to his feet to carry out the order. He ran into the kitchen and pulled down everything from the cupboard. The problem was that you can't make 'egg-fu-yang' without eggs. In desperation, San Mao deep fried a large pot of noodles, then he heated a large wok and stir fried all the ingredients he got out of the cupboard. Over the mixture, he added soy sauce and a large bowl of cornstarch thickened water. Finally, he served the fried noodles covered with the hodge-podge mixture of leftovers.

To San Mao's relief, the Viceroy ate the new concoction with gusto. The reporters also partook in the meal, which proved to be delicious. They asked the very much comforted San Mao, "What is that dish you cooked for the Imperial Ambassador?"

"**Chop Suey**," answered San Mao; *which is Cantonese for 'leftovers.'*

40
THE BEGGAR'S CHICKEN

Chinese cuisine is, arguably, the most renowned and popular form of dining in the world. The origin of individual dishes ranged from the traditional to the bizarre. The Beggar's Chicken was an exotic banquet dish that traced its beginning to the lowest caste of the society—the Beggars.

In ancient China, during one of the many famines that periodically ravaged the Land of the Dragon, refugees flooded into Chang Sho, a rich and fertile farming district on the outskirts of Hung Chou, in the eastern province of Kiang-Su. One refugee turned beggar, forced by a pang of hunger, snuck into a village and stole a chicken. Without cooking utensils and ingredients, he thought of an ingenious method to cook his meal.

At the bank of a stream, the beggar packed the chicken, feathers and all, in a thick coat of mud. He took pains to knead the mud between the feathers. A stick of reed, inserted into the chicken via its tail, decorated the mud ball. He then set the chicken to one side, as he gathered wood for a fire. When the fire turned logs into hot coals, he banked the fire and used a set of sticks to maneuver the mud-covered chicken into the bed of hot coals. Slowly, the heat turned the wet mud into hard clay. In time, a mouthwatering aroma wafted through the cracks of the clay and into the air. The beggar waited patiently until the internal juice of the chicken spurted out from the reed, indicating that the innards of the fowl were cooked. He then used sticks to fish the clay ball out of the fire. A deft swing with a stout stick and the brittle shell cracked open. When he removed the hardened crust, chicken feathers that had been kneaded into the mud also came off.

However, the poor beggar did not have time to enjoy his meal. The fragrance of his dinner attracted a passerby, who happened to be a servant sent by Master Sun, the owner of the chicken, to track down the lost fowl. Caught with part of the loot in his mouth, the beggar hung his head in shame as the servant dragged him back to the village.

In time, the servant presented the trembling culprit and the half-eaten chicken to the master of the manor. Master Sun prided himself to be a gourmet chef and had been upset at the loss of his prized hen; however, his demeanor changed, as he smelled the aroma of the chicken. He tentatively pinched off a piece of the meat and sampled it in his mouth. Then, to everyone's surprise, he sat down and consumed the rest of the evidence.

At length, Master Sun belched with satisfaction and gestured the beggar to come forward. The culprit cringed and fell to his knees, then shuffled forward to Master Sun. The beggar started to kowtow and plead for mercy, but Master Sun shushed the man into silence.

A week later, Master Sun invited a group of close friends for dinner. His guests arrived with anticipation, eager to taste the gastronomic delight of the Sun manor. They were surprised when servants placed a large terracotta ball, in a large wooden bowl, at the center of the table. Under the puzzled gaze of his audience, Master Sun picked up a large cleaver, and deftly struck the clay ball with the back of the big knife. The shell cracked open and steamy, fragrant aromas escaped into the room. Master Sun used the cleaver, assisted by a pair of chopsticks, to pry off the remaining shells. The guests were surprised to see chicken feathers attached to the inside of the terracotta skins. At a gesture from Master Sun, servants transferred the chicken to a clean plate and removed the wooden bowl along with its remaining contents.

With a flourish, Master Sun peeled off a piece of meat from the chicken and gestured for his guests join him in the dish. He then waited expectantly, as they gingerly obeyed his instruction. However, their skepticism turned to praise as they tasted the unusual dish. The host then regaled them with the tale of its origin. At the end of the story he presented his new chef, the beggar who stole the chicken, to the guests. Everyone congratulated Master Sun on his losing the chicken in such a fortuitous manner, and requested copies of the recipe.

The new owners of the recipe experimented with the crude instructions. Over time, generations of Chinese chefs refined the original simple recipe, culminating in an entrée on the Imperial Emperor's menu. Today, restaurants in Hung Chou City are especially well known for this gastronomic wonder.

Recipe

Ingredients:
- 1 whole chicken
- ½ cup soy sauce
- 2 cups Shao Shing (Chinese rice wine)
- 4 cloves
- 2 TBS ginger
- 2 TBS scallion
- 1 tsp garlic
- 1 TBS cooking oil
- 1 tsp salt
- 6 oz Chinese smoked ham
- ¼ cup Chinese mushrooms
- ¼ cup bamboo shoots
- 4 fresh lotus leaves
- 2 LB pork fat

Cooking Directions

1. Slice a hole in each of the chicken's armpit to clean and remove the innards. Wash and pat the chicken dry with a cloth, then remove the major leg, thigh and wing bones. Marinate the chicken with soy sauce, half cup of wine, ginger, garlic, and scallion for one hour.

2. Slice ham, chicken gizzard, chicken liver, mushrooms and bamboo shoots into long thin strips. Heat wok then add oil and salt. Stir-fry ham, chicken gizzard, and chicken liver then add mushrooms and bamboo shoots. Remove cooked mixture from the stove.

3. Stuff interior of chicken with stir-fried mixture (through armpit holes of the chicken). Pour in remaining marinating sauce. Place cloves at armpits and inner thighs, then tuck and fold chicken limbs onto the body. Cover with a thin sheet of pork fat, then wrap with lotus leaves and tie with hemp rope. Mix remainder of wine with mud, then coat chicken to form mud ball. Place in baking tray and bake over low heat (225 degrees) for three to four hours.

4. Remove chicken from oven. In presence of guests, crack and peel off clay shell, lotus leaves, and pork fat. Serve with pepper-salt. Be very careful when cracking clay shell to avoid injury from hot steam.

Culinary Notes

Modern Chinese restaurants serve Beggar's Chicken with a small gold mallet to break open the clay ball. Special care is required when cracking the shell, as the escaping steam and piping hot juice could cause injury. Customers keep the mallets as mementos of sampling such a famous dish. Some Chinese restaurants in the United States use a flour mixture in place of mud; however, this sanitary-minded substitute fails to approximate the earthy flavor of the recipe in its true form. The flour mixture tends to be stickier than mud, thus harder to handle. Flour also does not hold up as well under extended cooking time. It is also not as interesting a talking piece over the dinner table.

Health conscious connoisseurs could dispense with the use of pork fat in the recipe. In China and some parts of the U.S., people still can get live chicken at the marketplace, thus afford an authentic cooking process; however, with the advent of the modern supermarket, western chefs did not have to slice holes in the armpits to remove the innards of the chicken.

Traditionally, Chinese wineries sealed the mouths of wine vats with mud prior to storing them for aging. Chefs used the mud taken from wine vats, to prepare the Beggar's Chicken as a part of its marinating process. Since the average household seldom kept such mud on hand, wine mixed with ordinary mud became a part of the recipe.

41
THE LASTING PRAYER

China is a country based on a culture of philosophy. To the Chinese, religions are but divergent schools of philosophy, subject to debates over their merits and utility. Thus, it is no wonder that the combined total of all religious faithful number less than ten percent of that nation's population. Coincidentally, it also explains the relative few religious pogroms throughout Chinese history as compared to other countries. This anecdote sheds light on the Chinese mindset on the subject of theology.

Xiao Ma Fan was very upset. In a regimented society, discipline was taken for granted and accepted as the norm of daily life. At the completion of basic training, Private Xiao got a shocking surprise, he had been chosen to be a paratrooper and ordered to undergo airborne training. He was a conscript and must obey orders but he had no wish to jump out of a perfectly good airplane.

Political Officer Wang Yung noticed the young soldier's discomfort and summoned him for a discussion. When the young man arrived, Wang put on his caring visage. "Sit down private." The soldier gingerly sat on the edge of the rattan chair as the officer offered tea and cigarettes to put the trooper at ease.

"Private Xiao, I noticed that you appeared distressed. Is there anything I should know? Has anyone been mistreating you?" The youth shook his head in the negative and remained silent.

"Tell me your problem. Is there any bad news from your family or girlfriend? It is my job to take care of your welfare. I promise you there will be no repercussions against you for anything you say."

The private kept quiet for a few minutes then blurted, "I am afraid of heights, and now they want me to jump out of airplanes."

Wang grimaced then nodded in understanding, "I must admit, I too am afraid of heights." He smiled at the look of astonishment from the young man. "It is nothing to be ashamed of. But, instead of being afraid, you should be glad that the government presented you with an opportunity to overcome your natural phobia. We are all afraid of some things. By overcoming the fear, we become stronger, thus better prepared to face the challenges that await us in our future." He paused and then continued when Xiao Ma Fan didn't comment. "You know the government wants you to be successful, right?" As expected, the young soldier nodded in the affirmative, but remain close-mouthed.

"We have spent a lot of money to clothe, feed and take care of you. We don't want all that investment to go to waste do we?" Another nod. "You know the purpose of a parachute is to allow a man to jump out of an airplane and land safely on the ground, right?

"Now the government will give you a primary and a reserve chute, to ensure your safe landing." Wang noticed a slight ease of tension on the private's face. The Political Officer leaned forward and whispered, "You are a Buddhist, right?" He waved away the young soldier's budding protest,

"That's alright; I am not interested in your religious belief. So long as you are loyal to the ancestral land, you are safe from persecution.

"We Chinese are pragmatists if nothing else. We allow all religions to co-exist, so long as they do not advocate the overthrow of the government. My mother is a Buddhist, my father is a Christian, my wife is a Hui tribal woman of Muslim faith and I personally favor the Daoist naturalist philosophy. This reflects our basic Chinese mindset of being prepared for all contingencies. Just in case one god fails to protect us, we have backup systems in place to fend off the evil of all sorts." He paused for a slight chuckle at his own quip on religion and was rewarded with a reciprocal grin on the private's face.

"The reason that I brought up your religion is that, if both of your parachutes fail to deploy, you can always pray to Buddha to keep you safe. Now go pack your things." With lingering dubious doubt, the soldier rose, saluted and left.

A month later, Xiao Ma Fan struggled to force down his bile as he sat with his squad mates in the lumbering transport plane. He had breezed through the ground phase of the training with ease and now he faced the moment of truth—The Jump.

He followed the jump master's commands like an automaton. He did not remember standing and hooking up. One moment he was at the door of the plane and the next second he was falling through the air. He felt the jerk of the static line and glanced up to see the dark green silk wrapped up like the twisted fried breadstick he ate for breakfast.

He fought off the sinking feeling in the pit of his stomach and focused on his training. Looking up at the long strand of silk canvas, he slapped the quick release button on his chest and saw the chute fly away from him or, rather, he fell away from the parachute. Xiao took a deep breath and yanked the handle of the reserve chute, only to see the silk material pop out then collapsed back on itself.

He was running, or rather falling, out of options. Anxiety and fear enveloped him, but his Buddhist upbringing enabled him to accept his karma. Then, he remembered his discussion with Cadre Wang, the Political Officer; did not officer Wang suggest prayer? In desperation, Xiao Ma Fan clasped his palms together and chanted with reverent fervor, "Nan wu amih tou fou (Holy Buddha), Nan wu amih tou fou (Holy Buddha)…." as his body continued to tumble toward the ground.

In his fervent prayer, he sensed a warm glow and when he squinted opened his eyes he saw a giant green aura envelope his body. Then to his utter disbelief, a giant pair of green hands rose upward from a tall pagoda in the midst of the lush green hills. The hands formed a cradle as it climbed through the low clouds and caught the young trooper in mid-air then proceeded to descend slowly toward the ground.

Xiao Ma Fan crouched on all fours at the lip of the green palm that had just saved his life. He surveyed the beautiful green landscape and shouted with glee, "Jesus Christ! Ahhhh…." For, at that moment, the pair of green hands split apart then disappeared in a puff of green smoke.

THE END

ABOUT THE AUTHOR

Tang Long was the Honor Graduate of his class at the General Political Warfare College in Taiwan. He completed the Post Graduate Intelligence Program at the National Intelligence University, Bolling Air Force Base, MD, and had forty-four years of experience as a China Research Analyst/Subject Matter Expert for the US Department of Defense. He taught Chinese history and culture at Eckerd College in Saint Petersburg, FL, and is fluent in three dialects of Chinese and Spanish, as well as having a survival level proficiency in German and Japanese.

Other Books by Tang Long:

Tales of the Dragon – The Book of Lore
Tales of the Dragon – The Book of War
Pets Only (co-authored with Shadow Tang)

www.ingramcontent.com/pod-product-compliance
Lightning Source LLC
Chambersburg PA
CBHW071525040426
42452CB00008B/895